7/17/97

Robby, (that in itself makes you sound young!)

May this book make you feel as young as I am! Ha ha –

Happy 33rd Birthday,

Love,

Your Young girlfriend,

Young Jen

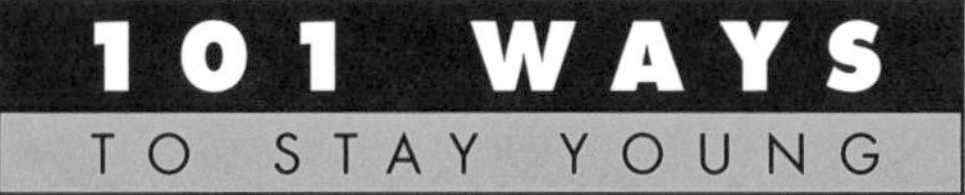

Judith Wilde and Richard Wilde

Warner Treasures is a trademark of
Warner Books, Inc.

Warner Books, Inc.
1271 Avenue of the Americas
New York, NY 10020

A Time Warner Company

Book design by
Judith Wilde and Richard Wilde
Illustrations by Richard Wilde
Written by Judith Wilde
Assistant designer: Doron Edut
Production by REI Media Group

Printed in Singapore.
First Printing: September 1995
10 9 8 7 6 5 4 3 2

ISBN: 0-446-91057-0

Please exercise caution when attempting any feats or activities in this book.

The authors and publisher are not responsible for any injuries incurred.

ACKNOWLEDGMENTS

Special thanks to the following people for their input, expertise and remembrances of childhood.

Aunt Joyce
Marshall Arisman
Sandy Balboza
Ed Benguiat
Rob Barrow
Rita Barnard
Michael Black
Gerardo Blumenkrantz
Jimmy Diresta
Doron Edut
Jack Endewelt
Mikel and Scott Freemon
Grandma Molly
Grandpa Robby
Mikey Gonzalez
Harvey-Jane Kowal
Zuki Landau
Dayna Levy
Fred and Jean Maltz
Ellen and Howard Margulies
Kevin and Susan O'Callaghan
Georgette Rosetti
Juan Santos
Ann Schwartz
Annie Thompson
Erica and Melissa Wilde
Brandon and Trilby Wilde

A grateful thank you to Jackie Merri Meyer, our editor, for being unafraid of looking foolish.

DEDICATION

Dedicated to Grandpa Robby, whose spirit of silliness lives in this book.

TABLE OF CONTENTS

INTRODUCTION

This book is a compilation of funny, silly, childlike, magical ideas, entertainments, inventions, and activities that we have done with and to our friends, peers, siblings, rivals, and enemies.

Many of these ideas come from a more innocent time. A time of less leisure and affluence that allowed for simpler creative invention. Or, the need to bring an object back to life, to make useful, to reinvent. Or, to discover, refine and perfect these amusements which are ultimately a form of expression.

The wish to learn how something is done results in the passing down of ideas from generation to generation which eventually enters the main stream, hence this book.

The authors have tried, tested, researched, and accomplished these ideas, inventions, feats, and activities in the truest spirit so that youth can be remembered and recaptured with the help of our friends.

1

SODA CAN SHOES

You will need two empty aluminum soda cans, and you must be wearing shoes.

Place one soda can on the ground, lying on its side. Then place your foot directly over the center of the can with its ends facing out.

Next stomp down hard on the can with your foot. As the center of the can flattens, both sides will cave in, firmly grasping your shoe. Do the same with the other can so that your feet match and you are wearing two soda can shoes.

As you walk and the cans scrape along the ground they make a most irritating sound.

Soda can shoes work best with shoes having large soles. It is a bit more difficult to accomplish with sneakers. Also, it is not advisable to wear your

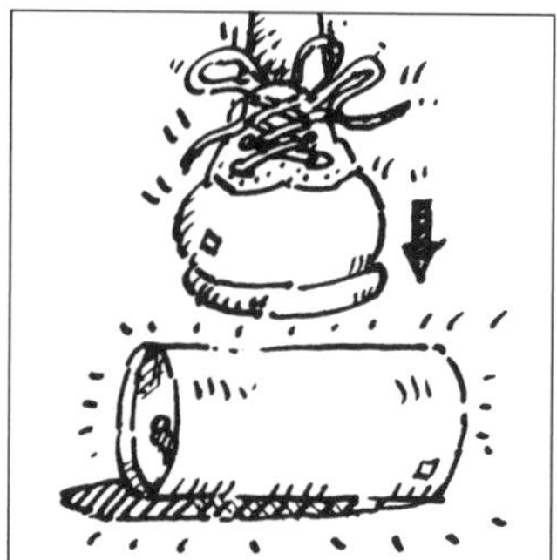

Sunday shoes. Do not attempt to do this in either bare feet or socks as crushed aluminum may have sharp edges.

To remove your soda can shoes simply push them off by stepping on them with the opposite foot.

2

CHICLETS™ BOX WHISTLE

Using an empty Chiclets™ box or a cellophane–wrapped candy box, either fold back or tear off the end flaps and place your mouth into the open end so that there is no space between the box and your face. Then blow. A high–pitched whistling sound will emerge.

3

FOIL BALL

To create a foil ball one simply needs to collect small pieces of aluminum foil.

Begin by squeezing the first piece of foil in your hand, compressing it as much as possible. The second piece gets wrapped around the first, the third gets wrapped around the second, and so on.

Keep patting the ball with both hands to make it round as you add layers.

Add as much as you can to make your ball as large as possible.

A wonderful aspect of making a foil ball is that it can go on forever. It is also a way of recycling.

4

INDEX CARD
PUPPET

To make an index card puppet, gently fold an index card in half lengthwise without making a fold line.

Then hold the sides with your thumb and middle fingers while you push against the center of the fold with your index finger. By squeezing the card with your thumb and middle finger, it will take on the appearance of a talking mouth.

The front opening edges are a good place to draw a top and bottom lip .

Now speak for your puppet.

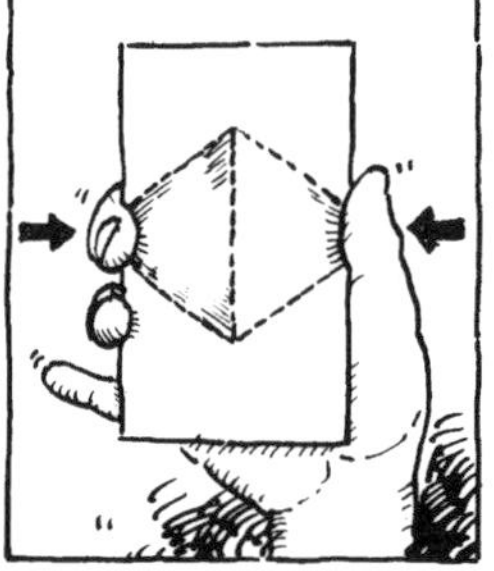

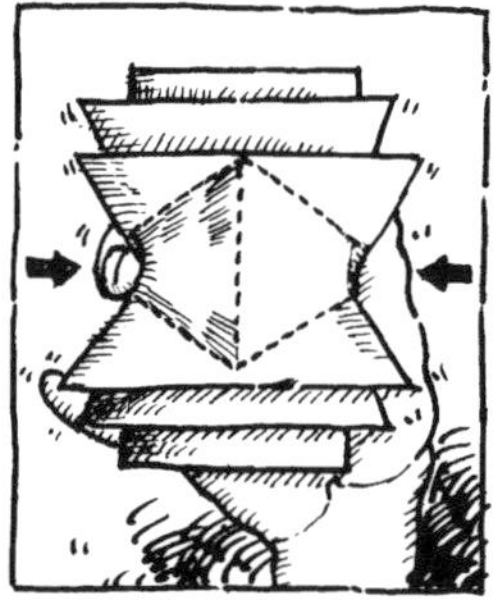

5

CIGAR BAND
RING

Cigar band rings are acquisitions.

First you must either know or be a cigar smoker. And second, you must acquire the paper band label that encircles the cigar and slides off easily. These usually have colorful and intricate designs and look great on your fingers.

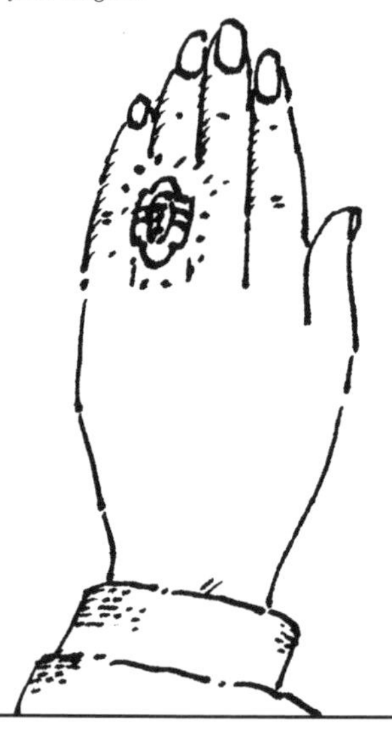

LIGHTNING BUGS
IN A JAR

Lightning bugs and fireflies are small, harmless night-flying beetles which signal to each other by emitting light. They can be found in abundance during the summer. Lightning bugs are slow-flying and therefore easy to catch.

Gently catch one in your cupped hands and transfer it to a jar with tiny openings in the lid for air. But be sure to release the lightning bug if it dims or it will die.

7

STRAW WRAPPER
CATERPILLAR

While holding a wrapped drinking straw in your hand, carefully tear off approximately a 1/2 inch from one end.

Slowly and gently push down the remaining wrapper until the entire straw is exposed, and you're left with only a squashed paper wrapper. Doing this resembles pushing your sock down to your ankle.

Next, remove the straw from the wrapper and place one finger over the opening at one end of the straw while placing the uncovered end into a glass of water. As you remove your finger from the covered end some water will enter the straw. Only a small amount of water is needed.

Replace your finger and lift the straw from the glass of water. Some water will remain in the straw.

Slowly remove your finger from the covered end allowing only a drop of water to fall onto the crumpled paper wrapper.

This will cause the wrapper to expand slowly, resembling the movement of a caterpillar or a wiggly worm. A second and third drop of water will expand the wrapper even further.

8

CARBONATED
DRINK SPRAY

Any canned or bottled carbonated beverage will suffice for this activity. Be aware that the results will be messy.

Begin by opening the lid of a carbonated beverage. Then cover the opening with your thumb and shake vigorously.

Once the drink is shaken it will erupt from its container with a spray and a sputter and an abundance of foam. By varying the opening with your thumb you can control the volume of the eruption.

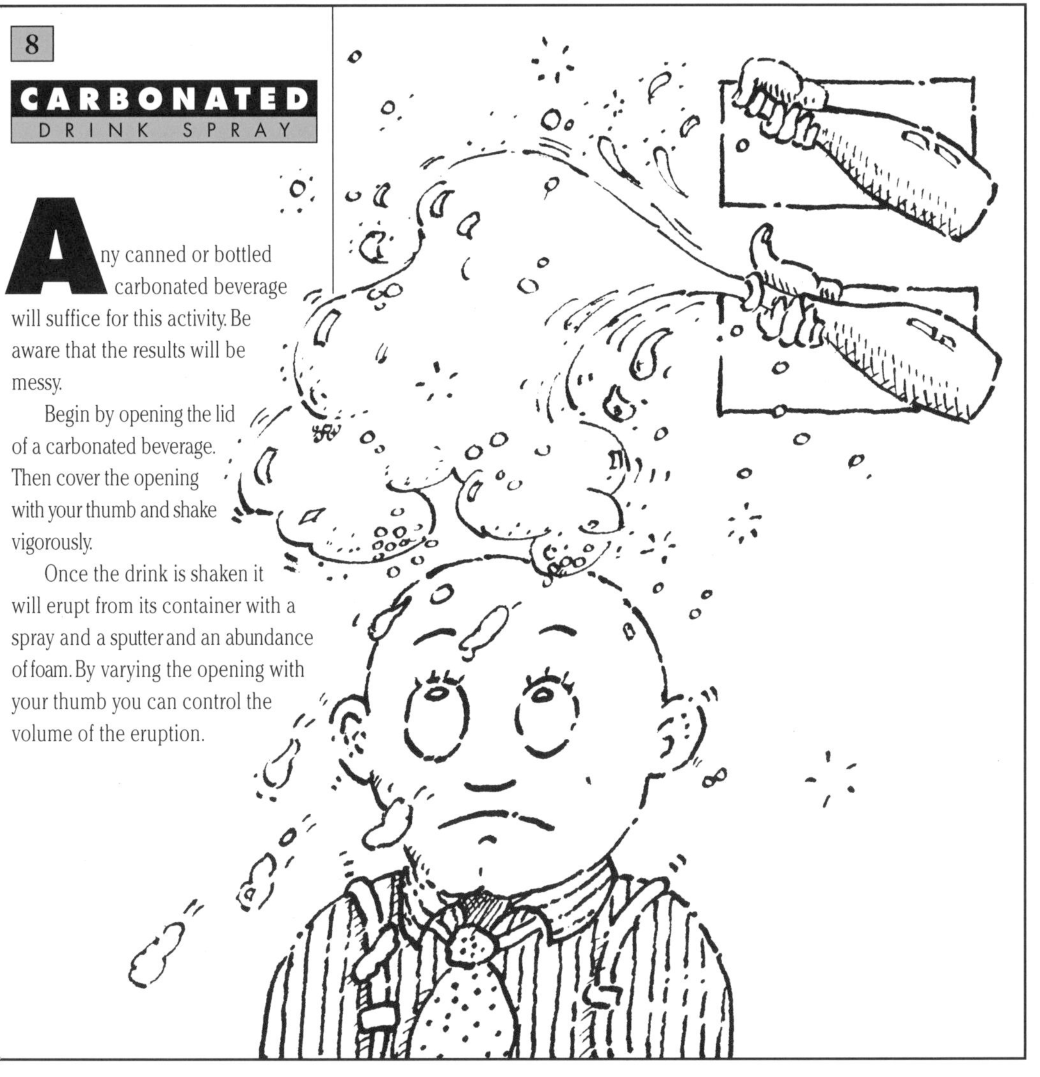

9

PAPER CLIP
JUMPING

Fold a dollar bill in thirds so that it mimics the shape of a **Z**.

Place a paper clip along the top edge of the bill, attaching the first third to the second third. Then place a second paper clip along the top edge as well, this time attaching the second fold of the bill to the last third.

When this has been done, hold the bill by its outside edges with one side in each hand. Pull the bill in a quick horizontal motion by moving your hands in opposite directions.

The paper clips will jump off the bill and join together.

Remember to stand a few feet from your audience so that no one gets hit by the jumping paper clips.

10

FLASHLIGHT
UNDER CHIN

Turn on a flashlight and point it toward the ceiling. Place it beneath your chin approximately two inches away.

The light shining from below catches on your features creating a scary face that you probably will not recognize.

11

FAKE
SNEEZE

Mastering this technique requires a true sense of the dramatic and the disgusting.

Practice your sneezing sounds in private. Then when in a restaurant or wherever there is a source of water available dip your fingers discreetly into some water while standing behind your targeted person, and pretend to sneeze loudly, "Ah-choo," while simultaneously squirting your victim with water by flicking your damp fingers toward the back of his or her neck.

The victim's reaction is bound to be an unpleasant one, so be prepared to apologize quickly and divulge what you have actually done.

BACKWARDS
GLASSES

Put either a pair of sunglasses or eyeglasses on the back of your head by placing the ear pieces over your ears backward.

Then turn your back on your audience.

As an alternative, if you have long hair you can push all your hair forward so that it covers your face and then put on your eyeglasses as usual, but over your hair.

Then face your audience.

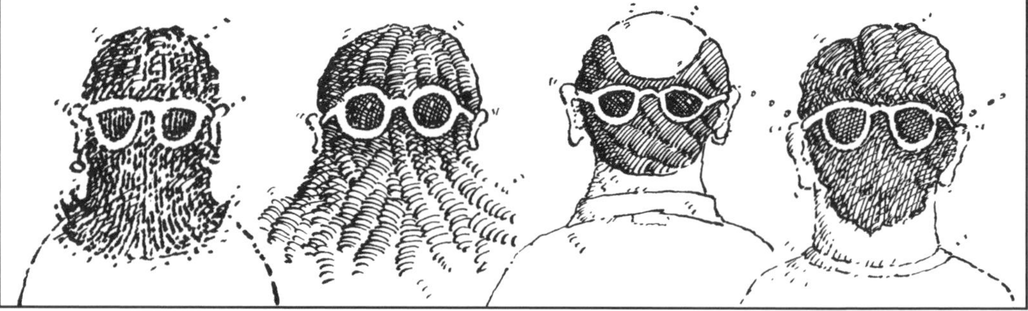

13

L7
A. K. A. SQUARE

"■" Hold both of your hands with your thumbs at a right angle to your index finger, which is pointing straight out. Simultaneously fold down your middle and ring fingers and pinkie into your palm.

Maintaining this position, place your hands together with your thumb and index fingers touching one another.

The space that is formed between your fingers is a square and signals that very message to whomever you're facing.

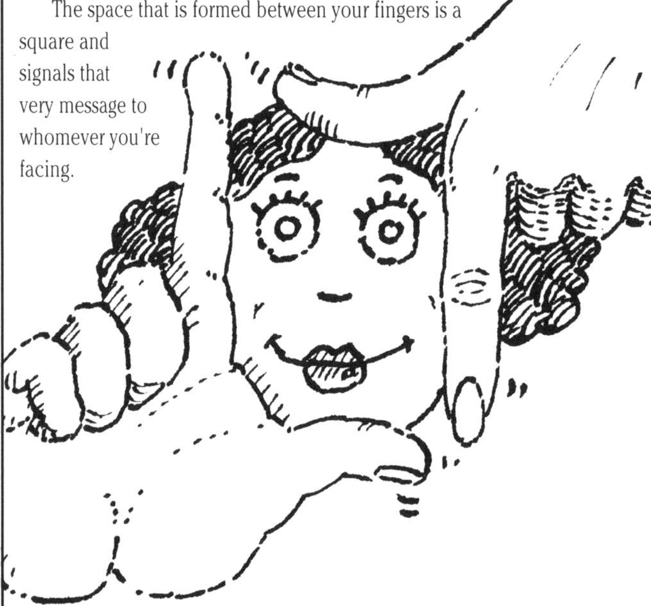

14

BROKEN
FINGER

This illusion must be practiced many times in front of a mirror to insure proper positioning.

Hold your left hand with your fingers extended and your palm facing your body. Bend your index finger at the knuckle and keep it folded in toward your body so that it appears as if your finger is partly missing.

Bend the thumb of your right hand and place it on the bent knuckle of your left pointer so that the right-hand thumb looks as if it's part of the left hand's index finger.

Then put the right-hand index finger or middle finger or both, depending on your dexterity, over the joint where the right thumb rests on the folded left-hand index finger.

Next slide your right-hand thumb away from your left hand and bring it back again, while it rests on the middle finger of the left hand. Repeating this motion will create the illusion that your index finger is broken in half and can be removed and replaced again and again.

The broken finger trick can also be executed by substituting the thumb as the broken finger rather than the index finger. This does however require more flexibility and dexterity. To do this, follow the above directions but do not bend your index finger. Bend your thumb at the knuckle before the nail so that the tip of it is not seen by your audience. Proceed as before only this time your right thumb will be resting on your index finger.

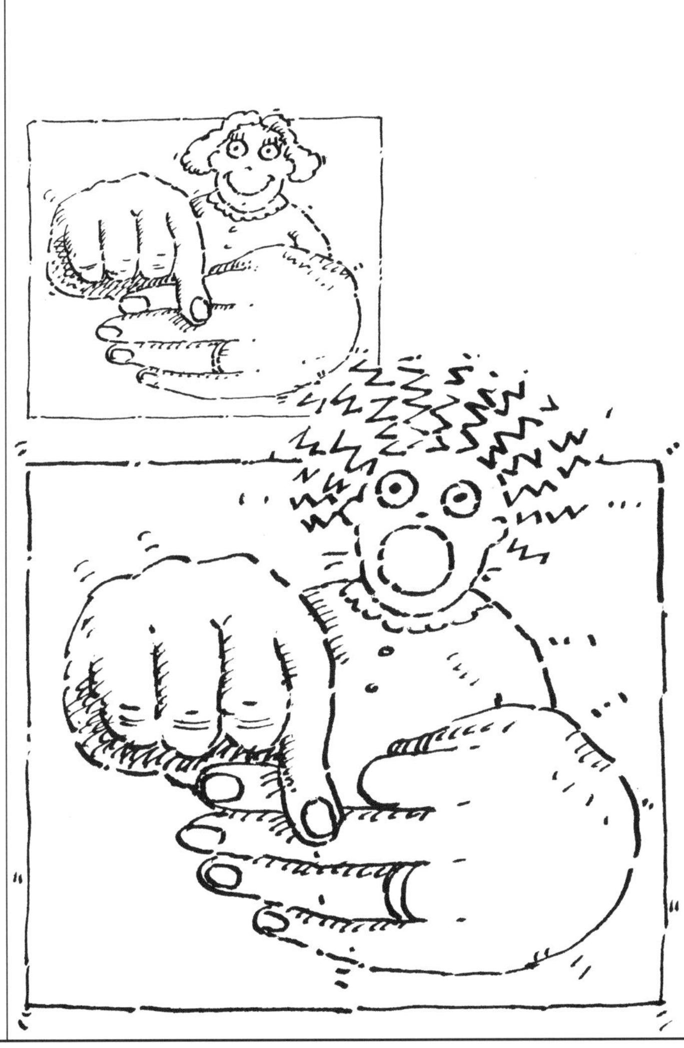

NAPKIN
BRA

The making of a napkin bra requires the use of any ordinary dinner napkin. Due to the fragility of paper, the napkin of choice is fabric.

Fold the napkin lengthwise in half to make a fold line. Then open the napkin and using the fold line for guidance fold each side of the napkin in half up to the fold line.

Next lie the napkin face down on the folded side. Then fold it in half forming a square so that half of the folded side is now on top.

Now comes the tricky part. Grasp the napkin by its four corners, holding the corners marked **A** and **B** with one hand and **C** and **D** with the other hand. Then gently pull your hands in opposite directions. The napkin will form itself into a bra.

SHIRT
BEHIND HEAD

When the weather is warm and while you are wearing a T-shirt, slip the front of the shirt up and over your head so that it rests on the back of your neck while your arms remain in the sleeves.

This creates a chest-baring look where men appear macho and women look very daring.

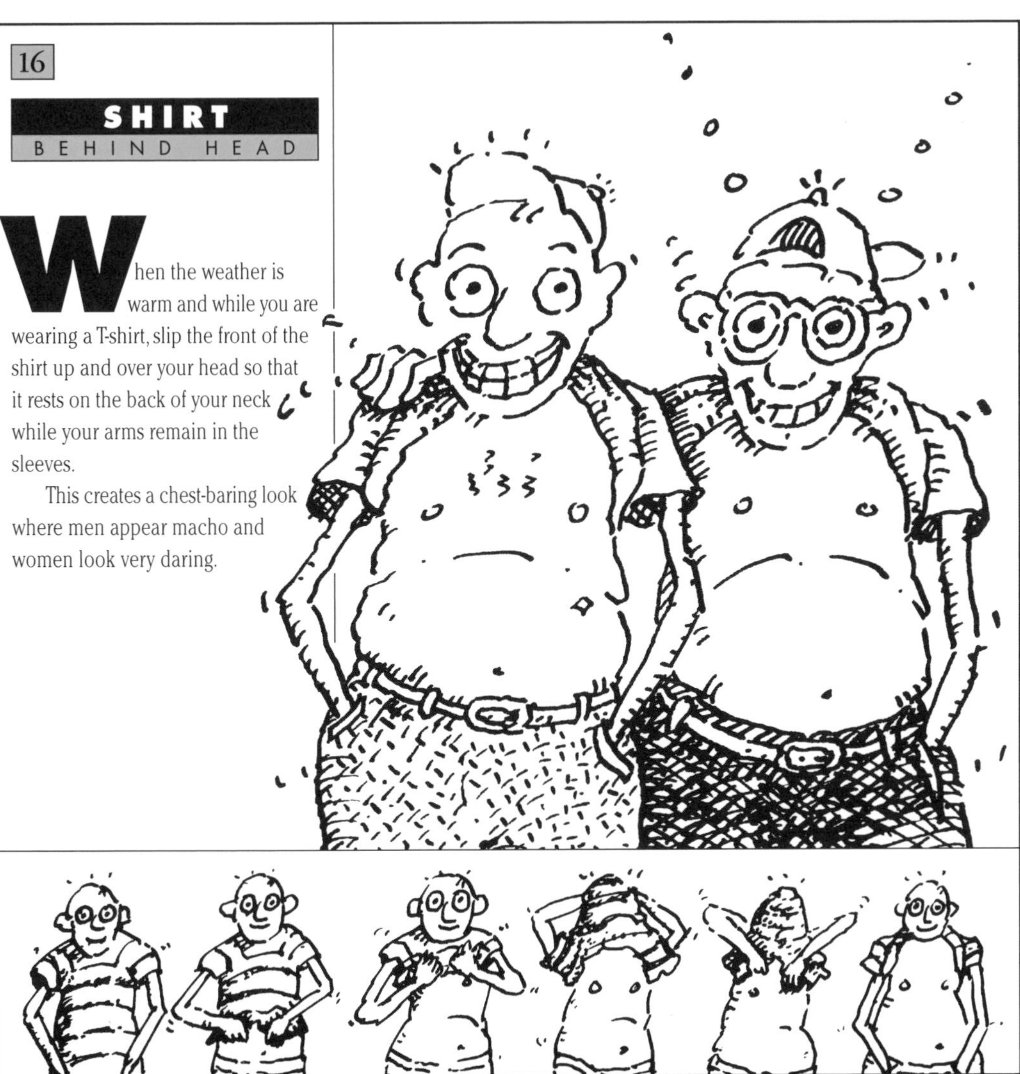

TONGUE THROUGH PHOTO

When you are perusing your favorite magazine, find a large photograph of a person or animal. The size closest to your actual head size usually works best.

Then using either a single-edge razor blade, scissors, or if need be your fingernail cut a slit between the top and bottom lips in the photo. With the photo facing your viewer, hold the page in front of your face and insert your tongue through the slit you have created.

The initial impression is quite shocking and can be used for an impromptu mask.

DOUBLE BUBBLE

Chew a piece of bubble gum until it is soft and pliable. Then using your teeth and tongue form it into a wad which you will place behind your front teeth.

Push into the wad of gum with your tongue so that you are sticking out your tongue and blowing at the same time. Do not use the entire wad of gum.

This will form a bubble. While the bubble is protruding from your mouth, repeat the step of pushing your tongue into the wad of gum behind your teeth and blow again.

A second bubble will form inside the first one.

WATER SQUIRTING

Cup your hands together with your palms facing one another and your fingers overlapping the opposite hand. Leave a small opening where your thumbs overlap.

Then dip your hands into the water, filling them. Next push your palms against each other, which will force the water to squirt out of the opening between your thumbs.

In a lake or ocean you can tell the person you're swimming with that you've caught a small fish in your cupped hands and as they lean in for a closer look, squirt them in the face.

20

RUBBER BAND BALL

Making a rubber band ball is a building activity that involves adding the same material again and again. It requires dexterity plus a certain amount of patience.

Begin by knotting a rubber band up by itself, making it as round as possible. Then add an additional rubber band by encircling and twisting repeatedly until it is wrapped tightly around the one which preceded it. Each new rubber band should be placed and wrapped in the opposite direction of the one preceding it. Repeat this exact motion over and over with each rubber band that you add.

A second way of beginning a rubber band ball is to include a small ball with a one–inch diameter at its core, prior to the encircling and twisting of additional rubber bands.

It may take as many as six rubber bands before your ball appears to grow round. Many balls begin as an elliptical shape but eventually with perseverance they do round off.

Consider beginning with smaller, thinner rubber bands, or if these are not available, double the rubber bands at first by folding each rubber band in half before beginning the encircling and twisting motion.

Rubber band sizes and colors vary greatly; they can be used in any combination imaginable.

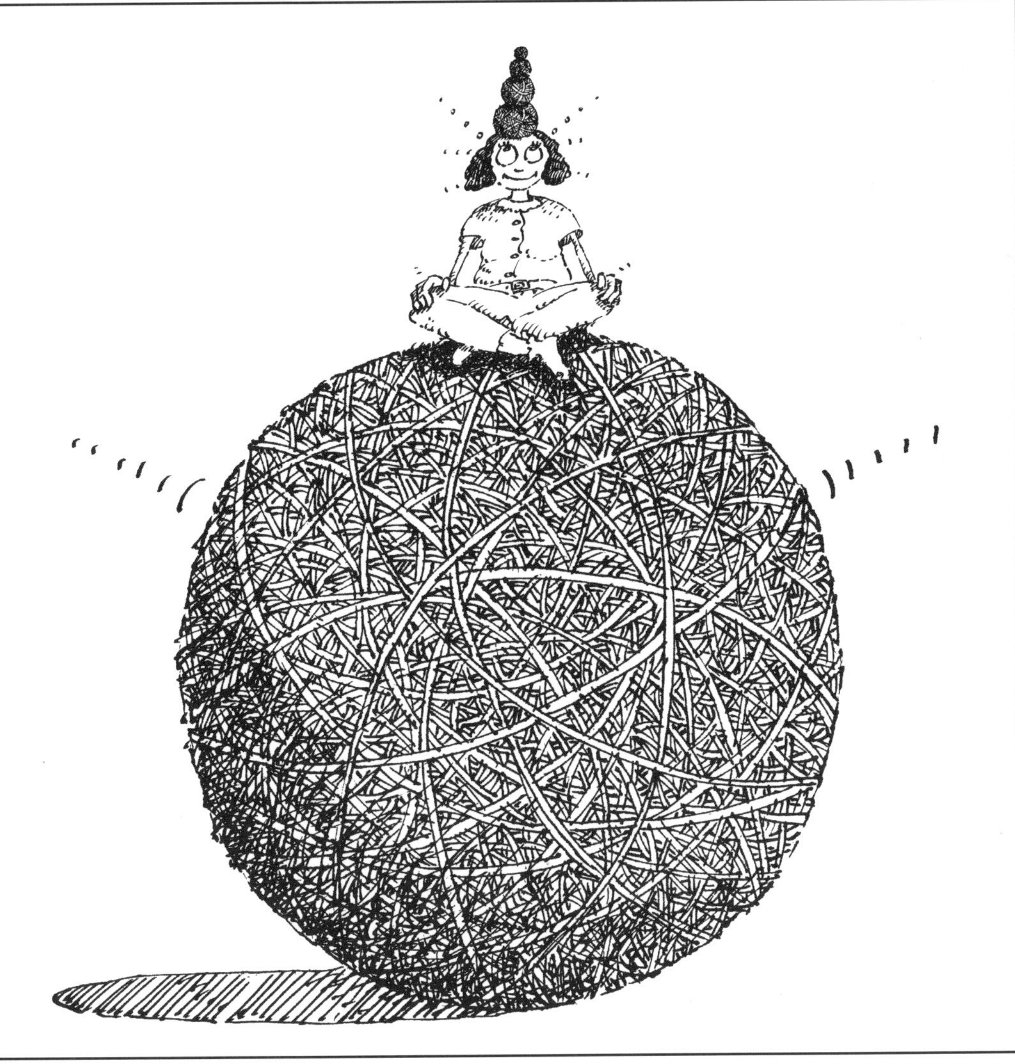

21

UPSIDE-DOWN
DOLLAR BILL

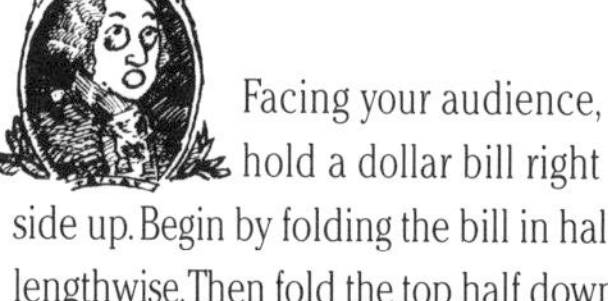

Facing your audience, hold a dollar bill right side up. Begin by folding the bill in half lengthwise. Then fold the top half down toward yourself.

Then starting from the front of the bill, opening the folded side upward, open the bill in its entirety.

The dollar bill will magically be facing upside-down.

22

BUBBLING
MILK

To do this, one needs a glass partially filled with milk and a drinking straw.

Blow into the drinking straw while it is submerged in the glass of milk.

The air will cause bubbles to form in the glass of milk. The more you blow, the more bubbles you will produce.

FAKE
HUG

With your back facing your audience, place your arms across your chest with your hands against your back, palms touching your back.

Move your hands up and down your sides vertically. To the viewer it will appear as if you're being hugged.

Making kissing sounds enhances the overall effect of the fake hug.

EMPTY GUM
WRAPPER

When you have a stick of gum, remove it very carefully from its wrappings.

Then reconstruct the wrapper by putting the foil carefully back inside the paper wrapper without the gum.

Next offer the piece of gum to your friend, who is bound to feel puzzled and unfulfilled.

It is nice to have an extra piece of gum available to dispel the disappointment.

25

NOSE
CRACKING

Cup your hands together surrounding your nose and discreetly put your thumb into your mouth, while placing your thumbnail directly behind your front teeth.

Pretend to crack your nose by rotating your hands slightly to the right and to the left while simultaneously pulling your fingernail forward against your front teeth to make a cracking noise. For the most believable results, pull your fingernail forward only once for each time you shift the direction of your hands. Do not overdo the sound effect.

To the viewer it will appear as if you actually cracked your nose.

RISING
ARM

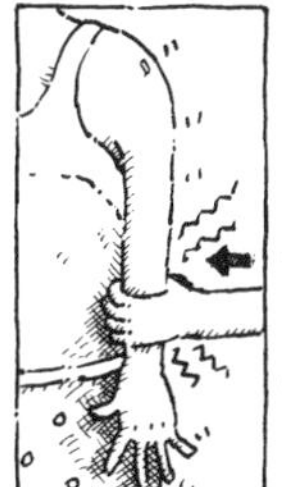

Have your subject hold his or her arm stiffly against his or her side while standing erect.

Next ask your subject to try to raise the arm while you hold it down. Both of you should be exerting as much pressure as possible. Do this for sixty seconds. Then both stop exerting pressure simultaneously, let go, and ask your subject to relax. Your subject's arm will miraculously raise itself.

27

HUMMING
GLASS

Dip your finger into a partially filled goblet or wine glass and rub it along the top edge of the glass in a circular motion (around and around). When you discover the exact motion and angle, the glass will begin to hum.

The sound will vary depending on the amount of water in the glass and the speed at which your finger is moving.

When several glasses are humming simultaneously, an eerie, annoying sound is created.

Keep in mind that this will not work on plastic.

28

BALLOON
ON WALL

Fill a balloon with air and tie the end by knotting it. Then rub the balloon vigorously against your clothing or hair. This will cause static electricity.

Now the balloon will adhere to almost any wall just by holding it against the wall and carefully letting go.

29

WISHBONE

WISHING

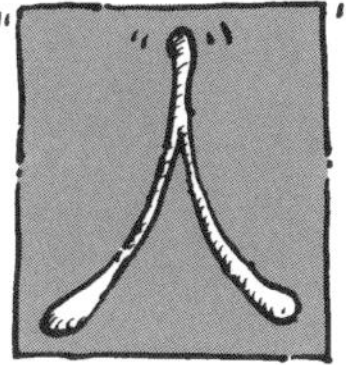

A wishbone is the forked bone found directly in front of the breast bone and may be gotten from most cooked fowl.

Turkeys provide the wishbone easiest to handle because of their large size.

After a turkey dinner, allow the wishbone to dry out. This usually takes twenty–four hours.

Then with another person, with each of you grasping the lower portion of a side of the wishbone, make a wish, and pull up and apart.

The person with the longer piece of bone remaining gets his or her wish granted.

FORTUNE TELLER

A square piece of paper that is approximately eight inches must be used. Begin by folding in each corner to the center of the paper, forming four equal triangles.

Then turn the paper over and fold down the four corners to the center of the paper, again forming four equal triangles.

Next turn the paper over. You will see four squares have been created. Insert your thumb and index fingers from both hands into these squares, pushing your fingers toward the inside corners. When held this way, the shape resembles a pyramid.

In this position you will be able to maneuver the four squares from side to side and back and forth, opening and closing them. This is the position for fortune telling.

Now lie your square down with the corners where you inserted your fingers facing up. Label these with the names of four different colors. Then turn the square over where there are eight sections. On these write eight different numbers. Finally open up this side to reveal the largest square. Here you will write eight separate fortunes.

Fortunes can be anything from "Kiss the fortune teller" to "You are going to marry a tall, dark, handsome man."

You are now ready to return your paper fortune teller to its triangular position. Insert your four fingers, and tell someone's fortune. Begin by asking your subject to select a color. Spell out the color as you open and close the fortune teller. Then ask your subject to select a number from those that are visible and count it out by opening and closing the fortune teller as you count. When you have finished, ask your subject to choose one of the numbers showing and read the fortune folded beneath the number.

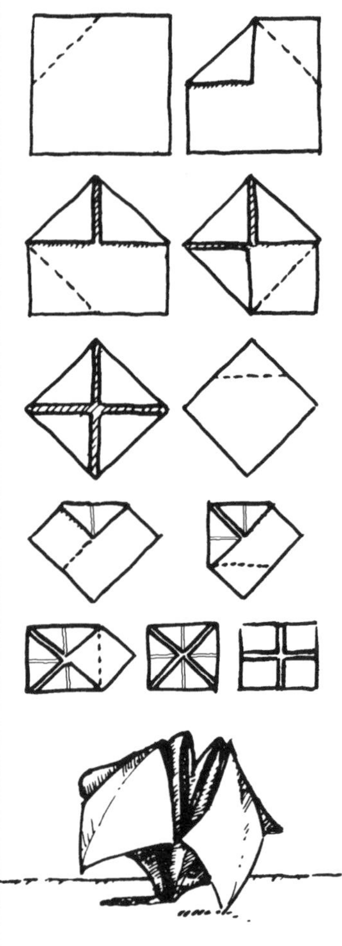

UPSIDE-DOWN
ICE CREAM CONE

31

It is hard to resist the challenge of eating an ice cream cone from the bottom up.

Bite off the bottom of your ice cream cone and eat it by sucking the ice cream out of the hole you have made in its bottom or by allowing it to drip down your throat.

If you can accomplish this without ruining your clothing you are a champion.

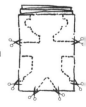

DANDELION
WISHING

32

Dandelions are common weeds with yellow flowers and grow wild everywhere. First you must find a dandelion flower that has gone to seed, which is what remains after the dandelion flower has bloomed. Next pick it, and holding it by its stem, make a wish and blow.

It is said that if you blow away all the seeds in one breath your wish will come true.

ELECTRIC
COMB

33

Run an ordinary comb through your hair several times. This will create a static electric field which will enable you to pick up small pieces of paper with your comb. The paper will then magically attach itself to your comb.

PAPER DOLL
CHAIN

34

Fold a piece of paper back and forth into an accordion shape. On the top section draw a symmetrical front view of a person with either their hands, feet, skirt hem, or hat touching both vertical edges of the paper.

Next carefully cut out the figure you've drawn while keeping the paper folded. When you have finished cutting, open the paper and you will find a chain of people, all connected by the body part of your choice.

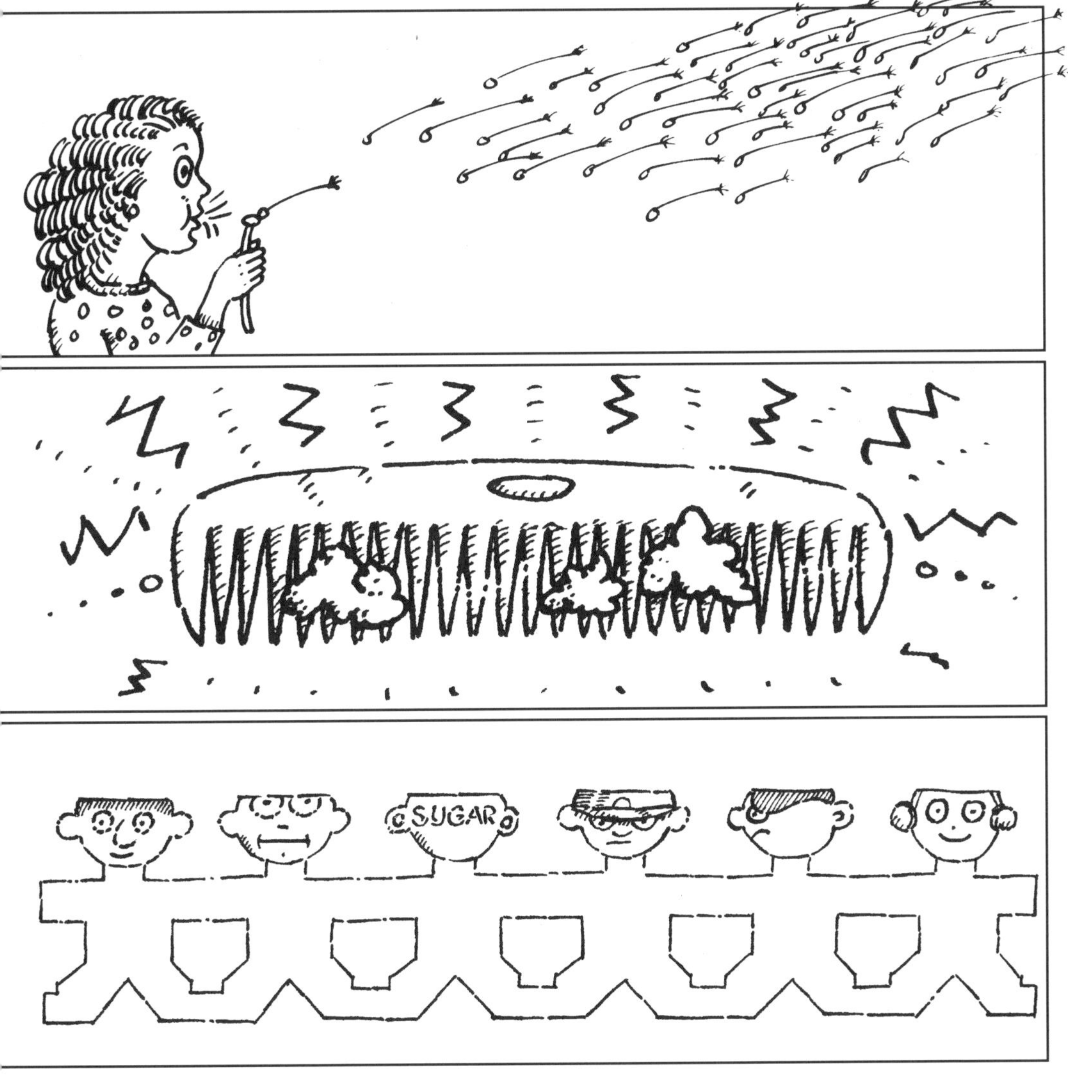
SUGAR

35

MISSING TOOTH

Brown paper candy wrappers or blackjack gum make excellent tooth coverings for make-believe missing teeth.

If using gum, you must first chew the gum until it becomes pliable. Only a small piece is necessary for each tooth. When the gum is pliable, cover the desired tooth by patting the gum into place.

If you are using a brown paper candy wrapper you must first dampen it in your mouth, also using only a small piece for each tooth. Then cover the desired tooth and pat it into place.

Both methods are equally effective and tend to stay in place for as long as needed, providing you don't eat. Enjoy the toothless look.

36

PENCIL MUSTACHE

Using an ordinary pencil, place it horizontally beneath your nose while forming your mouth in a pouting expression. The pencil, looking like a wooden mustache, will remain trapped between your nose and your upper lip for as long as you maintain this position.

FOOD GRINDER

Fill your mouth with an enormous amount of food and chew it very well. Do not swallow. Store the chewed food in your cheeks, chipmunk style.

Then pucker up and slowly begin to spew the food out while you turn

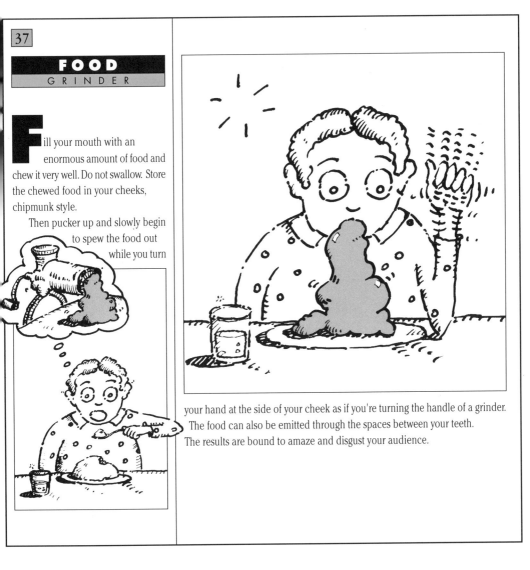

your hand at the side of your cheek as if you're turning the handle of a grinder.

The food can also be emitted through the spaces between your teeth. The results are bound to amaze and disgust your audience.

STRAW WRAPPER BLOWING

An unmannerly but playful way of attracting one's companion's attention. (This can only be executed with a paper–wrapped straw.)

Grasp a straw in one hand and tear off approximately a half-inch of the paper wrapper which covers the straw in order to expose one end of the straw.

Then slide the wrapper two inches down the straw.

Next twirl the sealed end of the wrapper. This is the head of the soon to be released projectile.

Hold the exposed end of the straw between your fingers and place your lips there. Do not allow lips or fingers to touch the paper wrapper.

Select a target—making sure to avoid the face and eyes of your intended victim—take a breath, and blow.

Enjoy the flight of your missile and the surprise that ensues.

Alternative Straw Wrapper Blowing Method

Follow the directions above but **do not** twirl the end of your straw wrapper.

Instead moisten the end that is sealed by placing it in your mouth.

Next aim for the ceiling directly above you. The straw wrapper will adhere to the ceiling because of its wet tip.

High school cafeterias are best remembered decorated in this fashion.

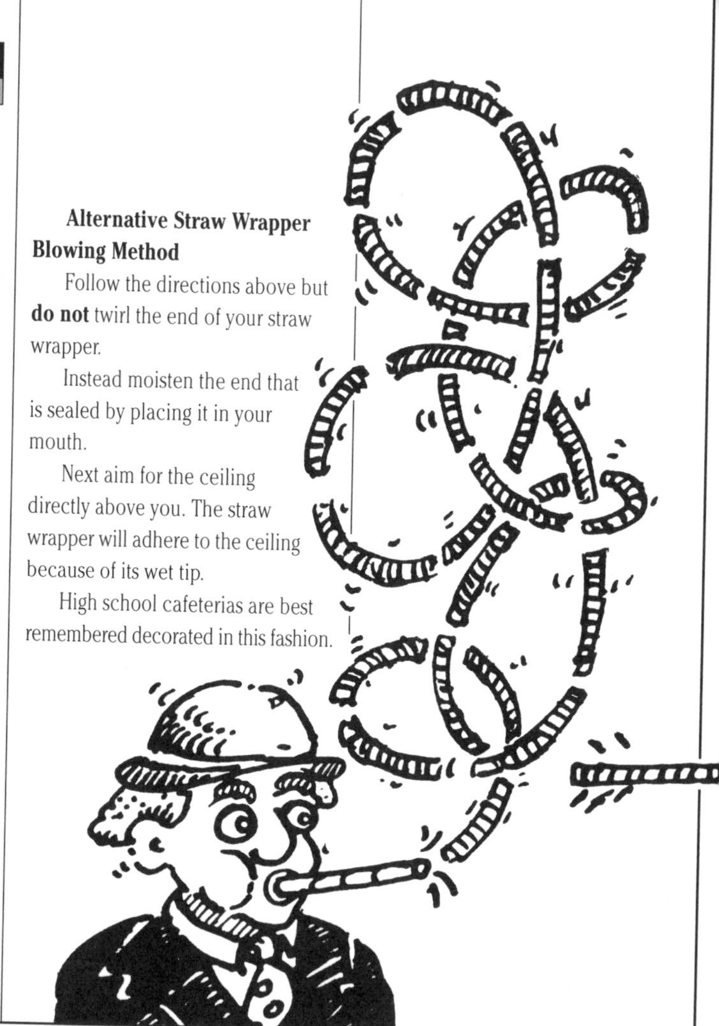

RUBBER BAND SHOOTER

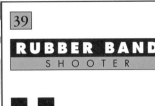

Hang a rubber band off your pinkie and fold your finger back so that the rubber band is caught between your pinkie and your palm. Fold back your middle and ring fingers as well, tucking them into your palm.

Pull the loose end of the rubber band toward you with your other hand and raise your thumb up while pointing your index finger. Then pull the rubber band around the base of your thumb and forward to attach it onto the end of your index finger.

Your rubber band shooter is now loaded. Find a target, making sure never to aim at a person's face.

To fire, release the rubber band by lifting your pinkie.

DONKEY
EARS

A particularly good way to choose your victim is by either standing next to or behind him or her while being photographed.

Then using your middle and index fingers to form the letter **V**, hold it over his or her head. Another version is to use your index finger and pinkie while your thumb holds down your middle and ring fingers.

If executed discreetly, no one will ever suspect your devilishness, at least not until they see the printed photographs.

SPOON
ON NOSE

Breathe on an ordinary teaspoon then hold it against your nose and carefully let go. The warmth of your breath will cause the spoon to remain on your nose without you holding it there.

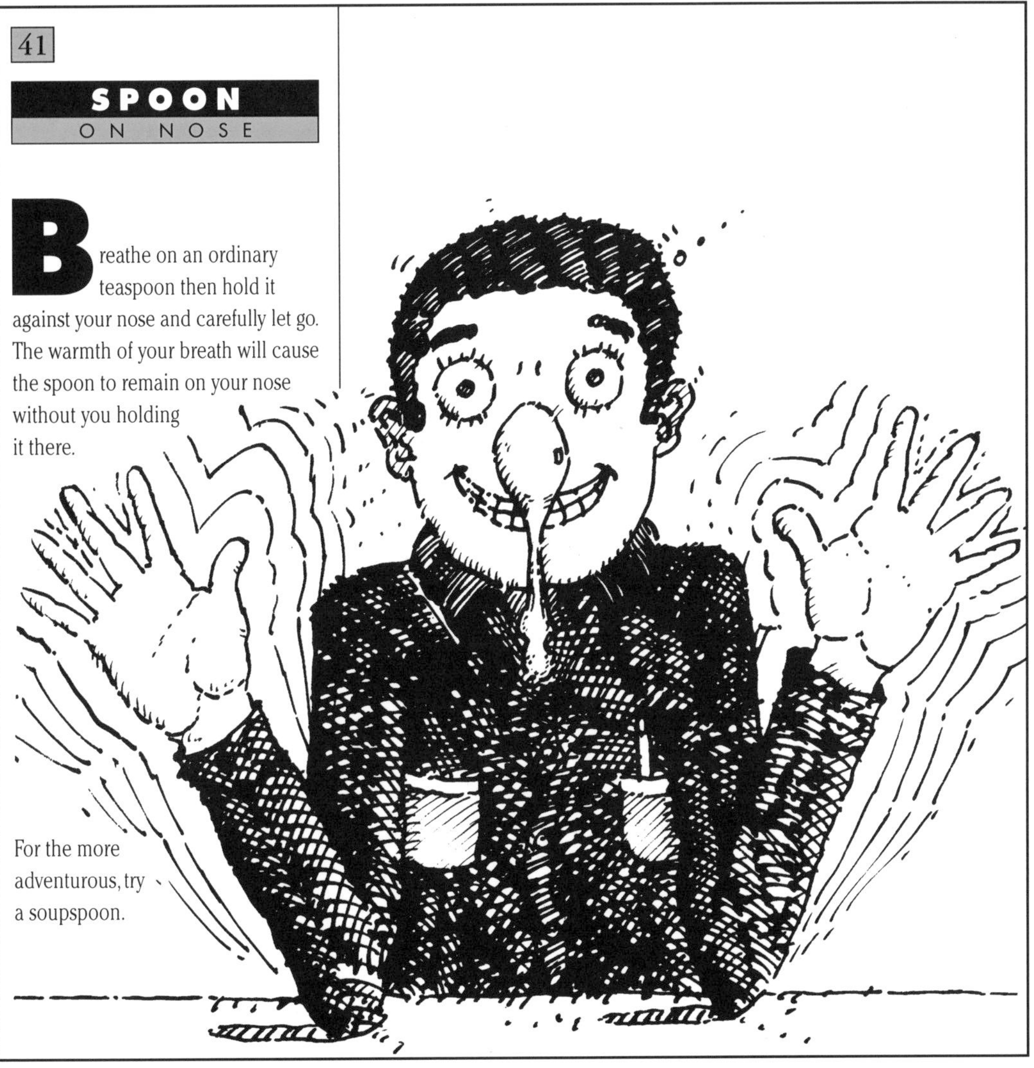

For the more adventurous, try a soupspoon.

FAKE ATTACK

Stand in a doorway or at the corner of a wall or building with your body only half-exposed to your audience.

Then using the arm which is concealed from your viewer, grab yourself around the neck and pull so that you disappear behind the wall. It will appear as if someone else is attacking you.

Use your visible hand to try to thwart off your attacker and sound effects to further convince the viewer and intensify the illusion.

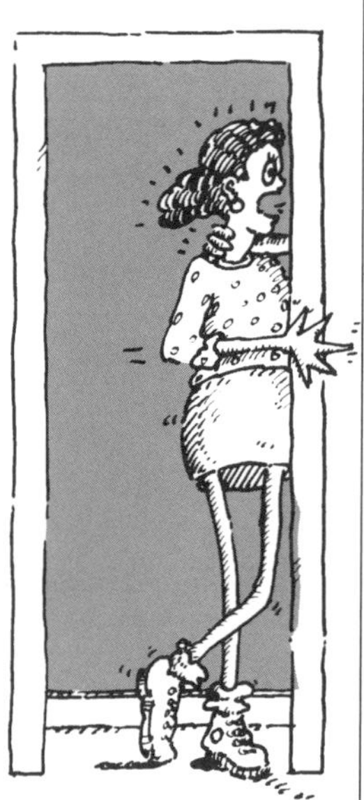

HALF DOLLAR
MONOCLE

Creating a half dollar monocle is done simply by closing one eye and placing a half dollar against your closed eyelid. Squeezing your eye tightly shut will hold the coin in place between your eyebrow and your cheek.

Make sure never to touch your eye with either your finger or the half dollar.

NECKTIE
THREAD

Using one hand, grasp someone's necktie near the bottom, by placing your thumb on the front side of the tie and your middle and index fingers on the reverse side.

Next say, "You have a loose thread on your tie. I'll fix it."

Place your other hand as if you're grabbing the imaginary thread. Your hands should be close to one another. Then squeezing the tie gently, so as not to damage it, roll it between your thumb (on the outside) and your index and middle fingers (on the reverse side) as you move your other hand away which is grasping the invisible thread.

Keep in mind that the hand holding the invisible thread never actually touches the tie nor would this be possible if neckties weren't at least two layers thick.

If done correctly, it will appear as if you are pulling out a crucial thread and ruining your friend's necktie.

45

CATCHING
LEAVES

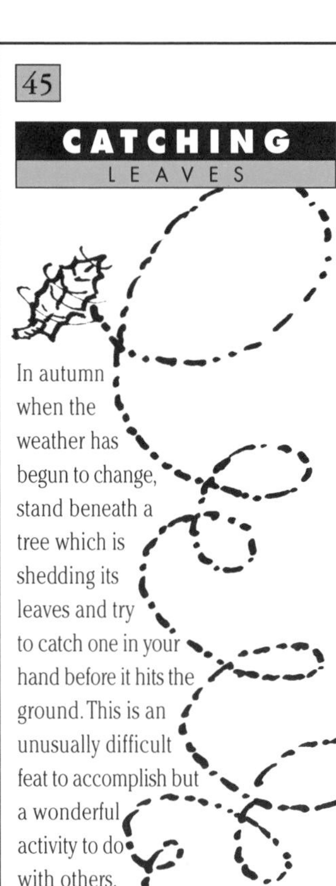

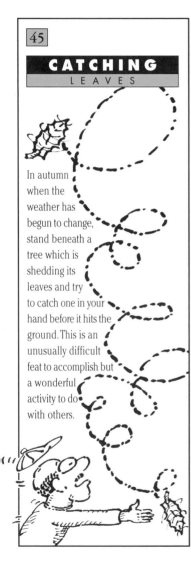

In autumn when the weather has begun to change, stand beneath a tree which is shedding its leaves and try to catch one in your hand before it hits the ground. This is an unusually difficult feat to accomplish but a wonderful activity to do with others.

46

ORANGE PEEL
TEETH

Cut an orange into quarters. After you've either eaten or removed the fruit, place the peel from one of the sections into your mouth, covering your teeth. This creates a mouth full of intensely orange teeth. This can also be accomplished with a lemon.

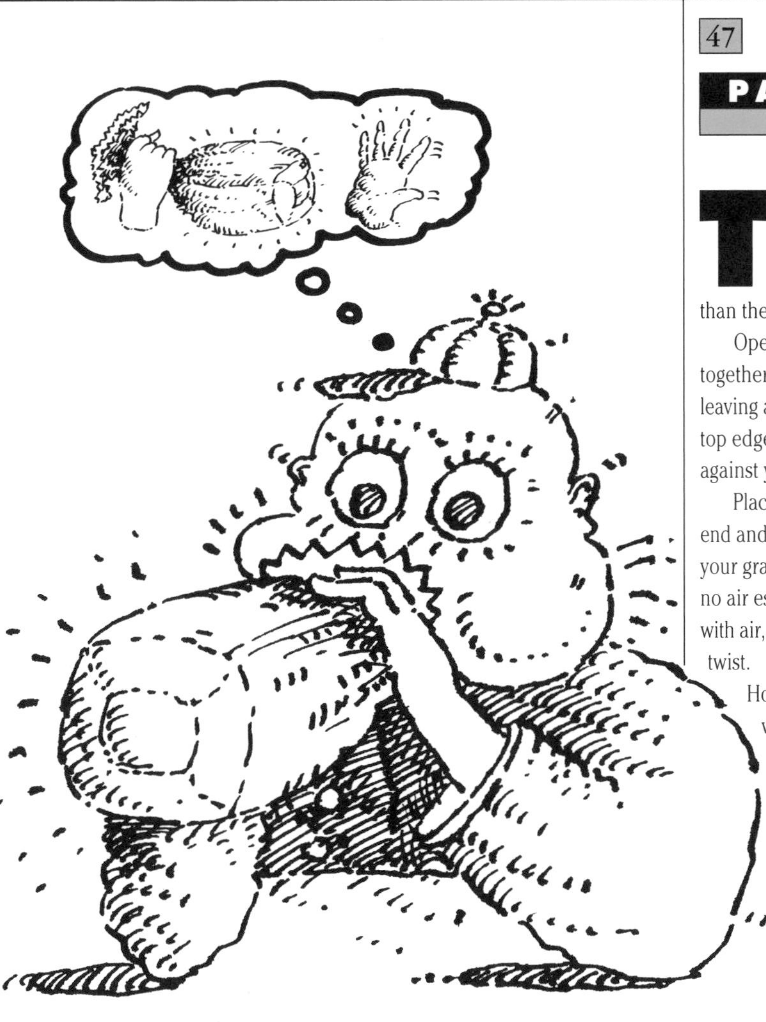

47

PAPER BAG
BLOWING

This is best done with a lunch-size brown paper bag rather than the supermarket-size.

Open the bag, then gather it together near the top edge while leaving a small opening. Fold back the top edge approximately two inches against your hand.

Place your mouth around the open end and blow. As the bag fills, tighten your grasp after each breath so that no air escapes. When the bag is filled with air, quickly squeeze the neck and twist.

Holding the neck tightly closed with one hand, clap the other hand firmly into the blown up bag. This will cause the bag to burst which makes a loud and alarming sound.

48

PENCIL
BREAKING

To break a pencil with one finger requires the participation of two people: one to break the pencil and the other to hold the pencil.

Have someone hold the eraser end of a pencil with one hand and the sharpened end with the other hand.

Then holding out your index finger, as if you were about to chop the pencil with it, raise your hand with the finger extended and move it up and down two or three times, as if giving a karate chop.

Next move your hand downward forcefully with your finger extended, but actually use the outside of your palm to break the pencil. To the viewer it will appear as though your finger has broken the pencil.

Consider giving a dramatic yell while executing this movement. It will enhance the splintering effect.

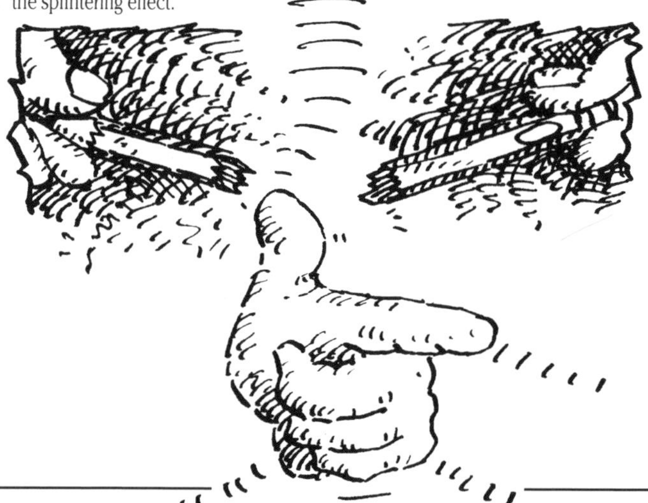

49

SPINNING
BUTTON

A large button with two holes is required in addition to approximately thirty-six inches of strong thread.*

Cut the thread in half and with one thread enter the button through one hole and exit through the other. Then with the other piece of thread do the same but this time enter and exit from the opposite side.

Next loosely knot the thread in place on each side of the button so that the button remains in the center of the thread with approximately a nine-inch double thread on each side.

Grasp one double set of threads in each hand and wind some of it around your fingers so that you have a good grip. Begin to spin the button by turning it as you would a jump rope or a handle. Always turn in the same direction. This winding up process takes approximately forty-five seconds.

Then, pull out horizontally with both hands. The button will begin to spin, traveling from side to side on the thread, as if the thread were elastic. This motion of the button resembles a yo-yo.

Continue moving your hands in and out so that the button repeats this motion for as long as you wish.

Eventually you will be able to walk the button along a table top or pass it to someone else.

*A large button with four holes may be used as well. Thread it diagonally from both directions and follow the directions given above.

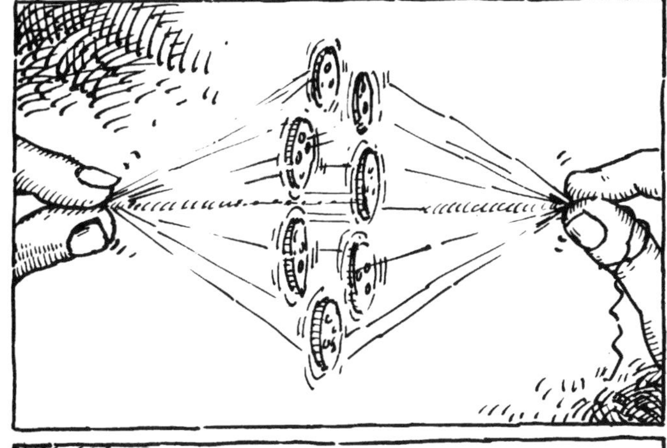

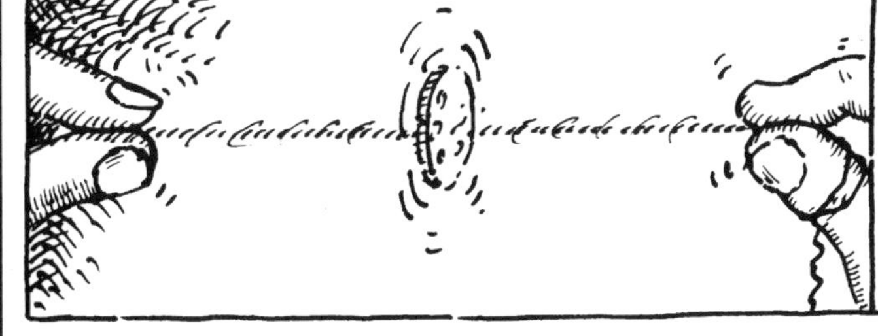

50

WEDGIE

When the elastic waistband of someone's underwear is visible it is the perfect opportunity to hoist up his underwear with either one or both hands by pulling it straight up along his back, which causes the underwear to bunch together forming a wedge in the center of his buttocks.

Consequently a wedgie is created which is uncomfortable, annoying and embarrassing.

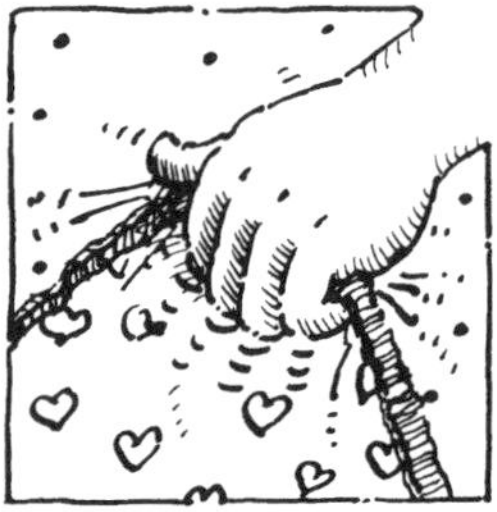

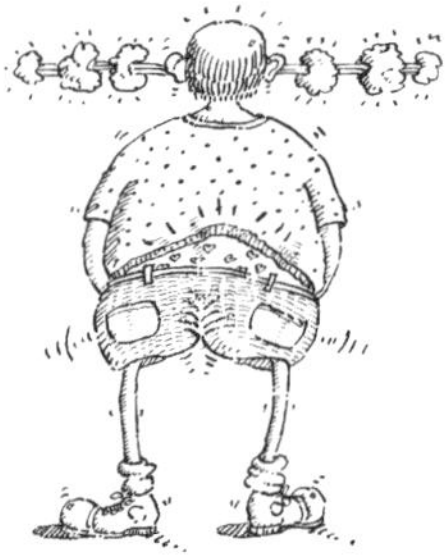

51

PAPER CLIP
NECKLACE

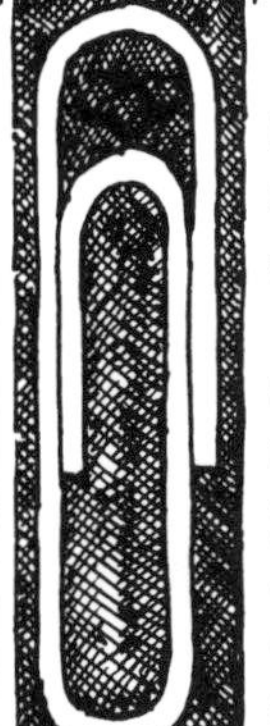

Making a paper clip necklace is one of life's simpler pleasures.

Back the curved end of a paper clip into the opening of another paper clip, and turn it around until it has entered the second section. Then pick up your next paper clip and repeat this motion.

This can be done rather effortlessly until you have formed a chain of a rather substantial length, or until you have exhausted your supply of paper clips.

52

SNOW
ANGEL

A snow angel is a way of creating a bit of heaven on earth. (Can only be executed in a snowy climate.)

Immediately following a new snow, locate a flat patch of snow-covered ground and lie down on your back with your arms at your sides and your legs together.

Next slowly raise your arms to shoulder height while keeping them stiffly against the ground. Then slowly return them to your sides.

Similarly extend your legs away from one another while keeping them stiffly against the ground. Then slowly return them to their original position.

Sit up carefully without disturbing any of the outer edges of the configuration.

Take a large jump to exit without disturbing the surrounding snow.

You are now a step closer to heaven than you were before.

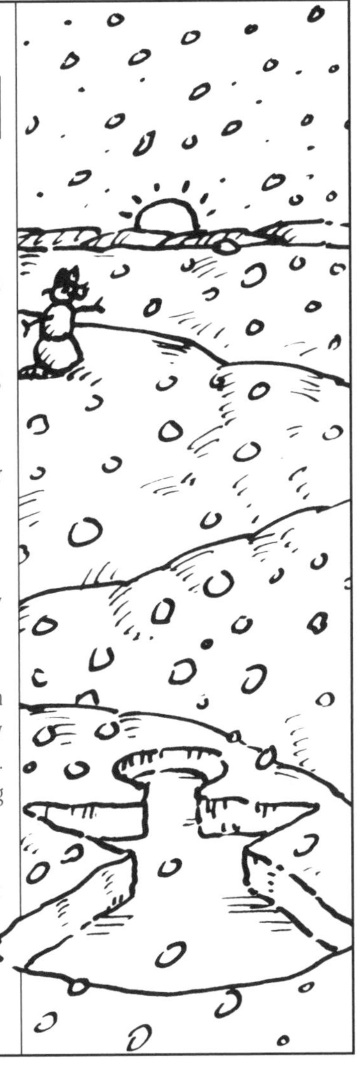

53

BOTTLE WHISTLE

To make a bottle whistle you need an empty glass bottle with a narrow opening and possibly some water.

To make a whistling sound place your bottom lip against the opening of the bottle and blow directly across the top or down into the bottle.

By adding different amounts of water you can alter the sound of the whistle. Adding more water raises the pitch. The larger the bottle, the deeper the sound.

The bottle whistle, at its deepest, sounds like a fog horn.

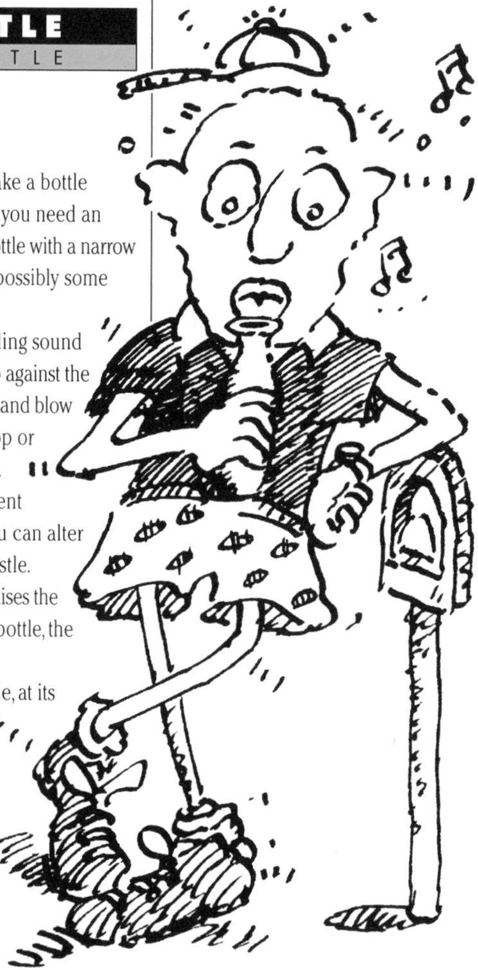

54

UPSIDE-DOWN FACE

It is easiest to create an upside-down face by lying down on your bed on your back and hanging your head over the edge of the bed near the floor.* But, before you do this you need to draw a pair of eyes on your chin.

Then using either your hair or your blanket, hide the upper portion of your head.

Next you need to call in your audience to witness your upside-down face.

*Do this carefully. Do not jerk your head back. Do not remain in this position for too long.

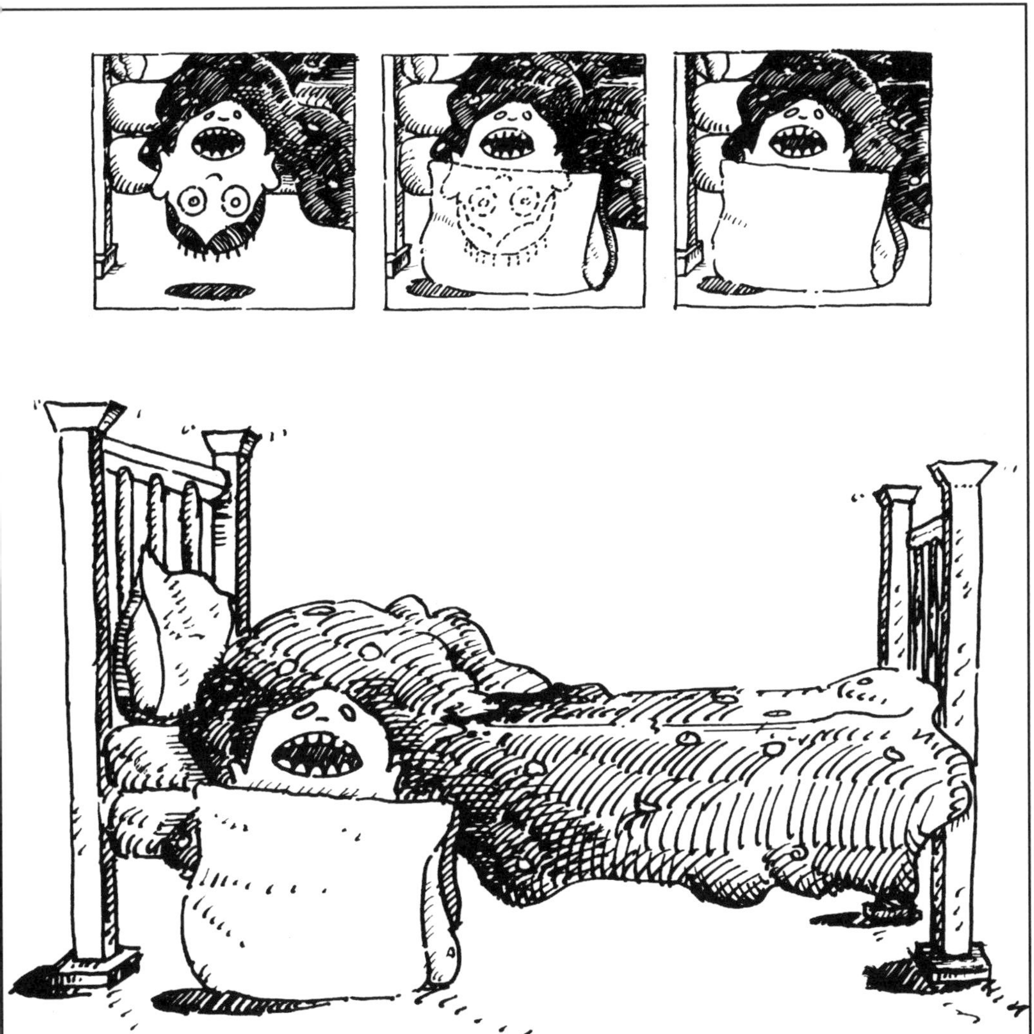

55

SCHOOL RING
SPINNING

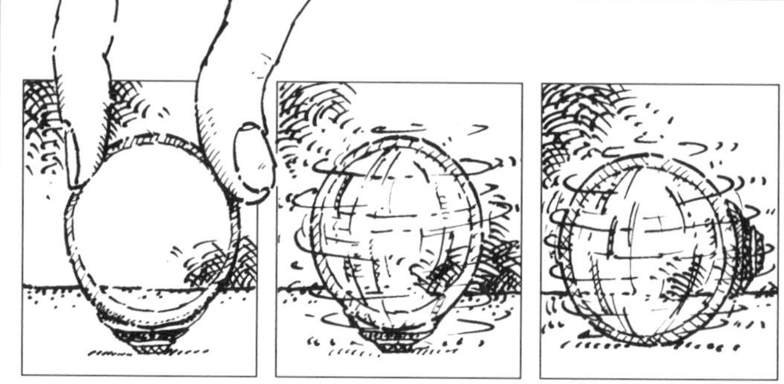

Hold a school ring face down on its stone setting on a table top and spin it hard by turning it using your thumb, index, and middle fingers.

If done correctly, the ring will magically flip itself over and spin like a top on the center of its band.

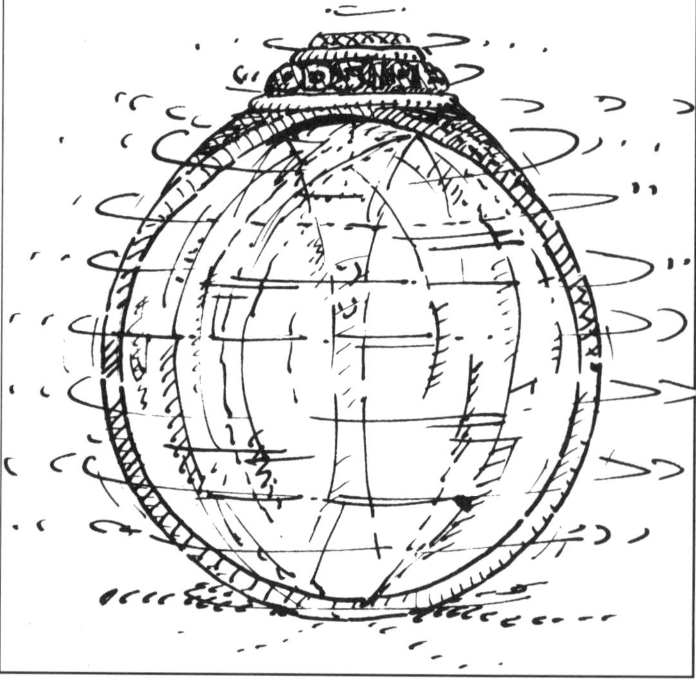

PAPER BAG
MASK

Take an ordinary brown paper bag and place it over your head. Once the bag is positioned, close your eyes and lightly touch where your eyes are with a marker, crayon, or chalk on the outside of the bag.

Remove the bag and cut openings where you have marked the eyes. This is the traditional paper bag mask.

Then put it on and enjoy the anonymity.

57

SHOULDER
TAP

When you are in a crowd or at a gathering, stand either alongside or directly behind the person you have chosen to annoy. While he is distracted, tap him on his far shoulder rather than on the shoulder closest to you.

Next he will turn to see who has tapped him, turning in the direction of the tapped shoulder. Seeing no one there, he will then turn back toward the other shoulder. You may then take the opportunity to (A) smile innocently and point out whomever you wish to be the culprit, or (B) simply turn away before the person looks in your direction and act like an innocent bystander.

Another method is to stand directly behind the targeted person, then immediately following the tap, kneel down directly behind him. People rarely bother to look down.

58

SHIRT
SPOT

Choose your victim and approach him face to face. Look down at his shirt in a concerned manner and in your most convincing style, touch a spot near the middle of his shirt, approximately midchest, and say something like, "Oh, you have a terrible spot" or "What's this on your shirt?"

As he is moving his head down to look, lift your finger and tap him on the bottom of his nose.

It works every time.

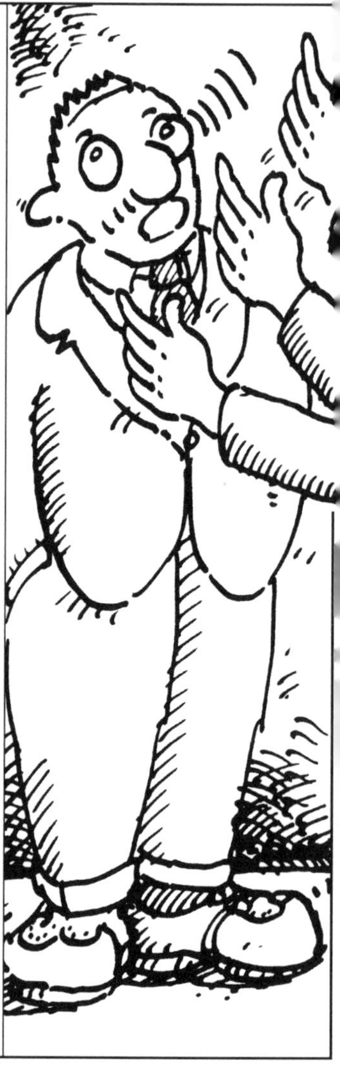

POLLYWOG
ON NOSE

Find a pollywog (maple seed). This usually isn't very difficult if there are maple trees around. From midsummer to late fall pollywogs are plentiful.

Insert your fingernail into the thick end of the pollywog and discard the seed. Next spread this thick end apart and place it on your nose.

The moistness inside will act as glue and usually the pollywog will remain in place as long as it's not accompanied by too much facial movement, such as a sneeze.

Pollywogs can also be placed on your fingernails, creating grotesquely ghoulish hands.

FISH
FACE

A fish face mimics the expression commonly seen on the face of a goldfish.

To make a fish face, suck in your cheeks and pucker your lips simultaneously.

Trying to kiss someone while maintaining this posture is the ultimate challenge.

61

TEARING
PAPER

Tearing paper is best done by either grabbing an important piece of paper from your subject, or when given a valuable piece of paper do the following:

Hold the paper in both hands by its top edge just below your chin while facing your subject. Pretend to tear the paper by sliding one hand down the center of the paper while blowing straight down against the top edge from front to back.

It is the blowing which produces the sound of paper tearing, which will both frighten and annoy your victim. The hand motion is for visual enhancement only. Be careful not to tear or damage the paper.

62

SQUEALING
BALLOON

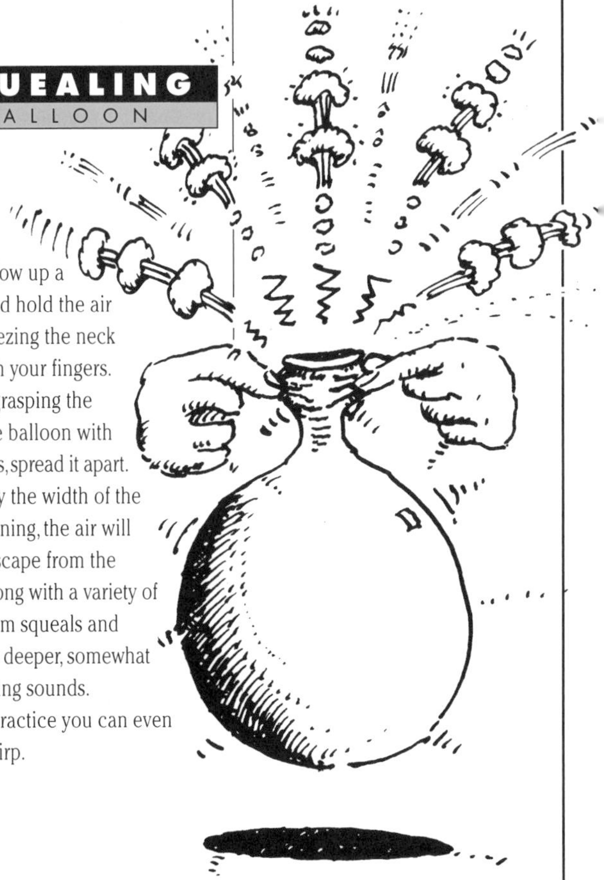

Blow up a balloon and hold the air in by squeezing the neck closed with your fingers.

Then grasping the neck of the balloon with your fingers, spread it apart. As you vary the width of the neck's opening, the air will begin to escape from the balloon along with a variety of sounds, from squeals and squeaks to deeper, somewhat embarrassing sounds.

With practice you can even make it chirp.

EYELASH
WISHING

When you lose an eyelash put it on your fingertip and touch it against your friend's fingertip.

Then you both make a wish and when you separate your fingers the person with the eyelash on their fingertip is the one whose wish will come true.

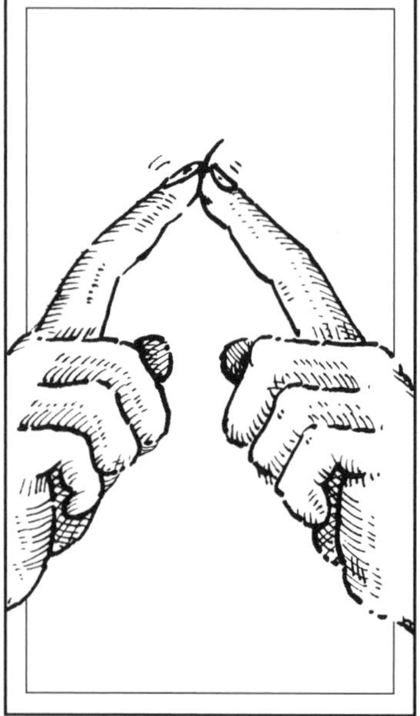

RUBBER
PENCIL

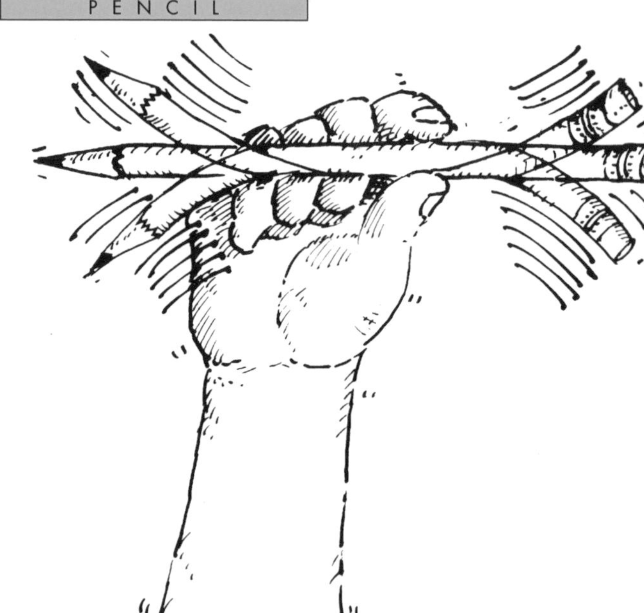

Hold an ordinary pencil slightly off-center between your thumb and index fingers. Keep the pencil horizontal and your grip very loose.

Shake the pencil with short movements by rapidly raising and lowering your arm. Move your arm no more than an inch in either direction. Be aware that a common mistake is to move the pencil with your fingers. Relax and allow the arm movement to create the desired effect.

If done correctly, the pencil will begin to wobble and appear rubbery.

65

FINGER
WHISTLING

Place your thumb and index finger together, forming an **0**. Next place these two fingers into your mouth pressing against the tip of your tongue as you curl your tongue back slightly, while pushing forward against your fingers at the same time.

Roll your lips tightly around your teeth while keeping your lips tensed. Do not relax your mouth but keep it slightly ajar. Take a deep breath and blow, making sure not to puff out your cheeks. If the whistle does not sound clear, maneuver your fingers slightly until you find the right position.

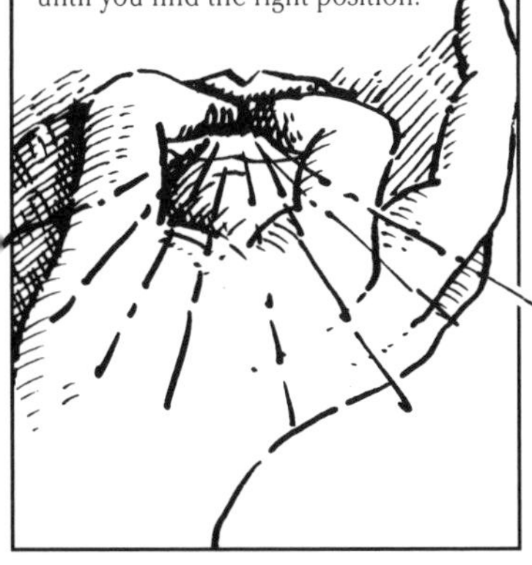

66

KAZOO
COMB

You will need an ordinary comb and a small piece of paper, approximately the same size as the comb or slightly smaller.

Begin by running a comb through your hair several times. This gathers static electricity which enables the paper to adhere to the comb.

Once this is accomplished, hold the comb horizontally, with your mouth against the side of the comb where the paper has attached itself, and hum.

This produces an exact replica of a kazoo's sound.

67

FINGER MOVING

This must be done with two people. So choose your subject.

Ask him to cross his arms in front of him with his palms touching.

Next have him clasp his hands and rotate his arms inward, so that he ends up with his hands clasped beneath his chin.

Then without touching your subject, point to a ring finger and ask him to move it without moving the rest of his fingers.

In this position your subject will rarely be able to control which finger he moves.

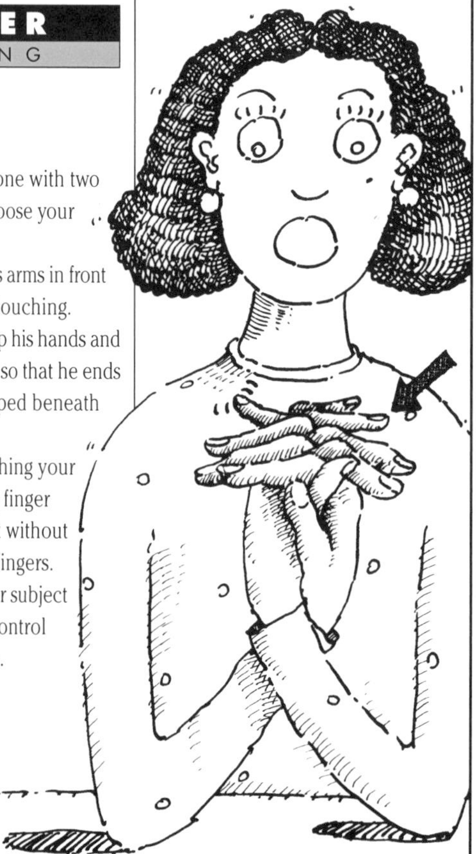

68

ARMPIT NOISES

Place your cupped hand directly under your armpit with your palm loosely against your upper chest. Your index finger should touch against the crease of your armpit and your thumb should rest against the front of your chest.

Then rapidly raise and lower your other arm in a winglike, flapping motion. After a few seconds your hand becomes suctioned to your body and as the air escapes some truly interesting noises will emerge from your armpit.

TIRE CAP
WHISTLE

A tire cap whistle requires the use of a tire cap. A tire cap is the very small screw-on cap found on automobile and bicycle tires that keeps the air from escaping.

After you have borrowed a tire cap, make a fist and position the cap between your middle and ring fingers, placing it as far back as possible with the open end facing out, leaving it partially exposed between your middle and ring fingers.

Then place your lips over your bent fingers with your mouth directly in the center of your middle and ring fingers and blow into the open end of the tire cap. Maneuver your mouth around until you find the perfect angle. A very high-pitched squeal will emanate.

70

WALRUS TUSK
CHOPSTICKS

Gently insert the narrow ends of a pair of chopsticks into your mouth between your upper lip and your top teeth.

The chopsticks will remain where you have positioned them unless you try to eat. They will resemble the tusks of a walrus. Grunting sounds are appropriate at this time.

71

"KICK ME"
SIGN

Write the message you wish to impart on a piece of paper.

Using adhesive tape, stick the sign to someone's back without him or her knowing. This is the difficult part. Consider using Post-It™ notes which eliminate the need for adhesive tape.

The best technique for doing this is to greet someone from behind and pat him or her on the back while attaching the sign. Another way is to stumble into your victim and attach the sign. Then quickly apologize for your clumsiness.

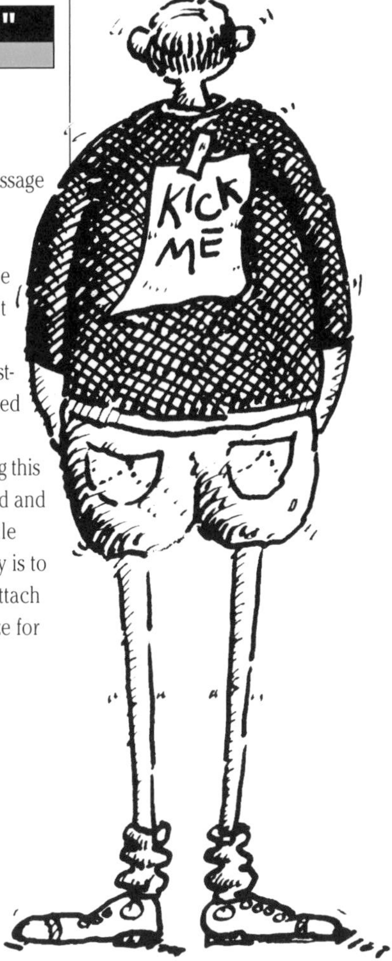

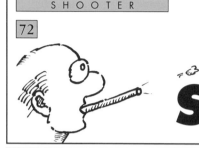

Spitballs, in this instance, are small wads of chewed paper that are shaped into balls that are spit at the bodies—never the faces—of one's peers and enemies alike.

To shoot a spitball, use a plastic drinking straw, or if a straw is not available,

CAN TELEPHONE

73

Choose either two empty cans with their lids removed or two empty paper cups to make a telephone. A piece of string approximately twelve feet long is also needed. Next puncture the bottom of either the cans or the cups and thread a string through the hole that you've made. Knot the string so that it stays inside the can and do the

SKIMMING STONES

74

Flat stones and a body of water are needed to accomplish this feat. If there are no flat stones available, a rounded stone will suffice, but make sure to give the rock a good spin upon its release.

Grasp the stone firmly with your thumb and index finger along its outside edge while

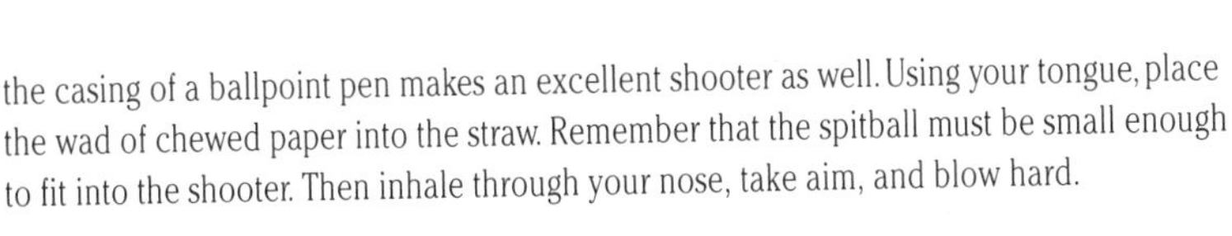

the casing of a ballpoint pen makes an excellent shooter as well. Using your tongue, place the wad of chewed paper into the straw. Remember that the spitball must be small enough to fit into the shooter. Then inhale through your nose, take aim, and blow hard.

same with the other end of the string so that the two cans are connected.

Stand holding one can with the string taut while your friend holds the other can.

One person talks into his or her can while the other person holds the can against his or her ear. You cannot speak at the same time but must take turns.

keeping its flat side parallel to the ground.

A side-arm toss is most effective for skimming the stone. Release the stone by spinning it off your index finger, propelling it parallel to the ground. The stone must land on the water with its nose slightly uplifted.

As you become more proficient, the challenge is to see how many times you can make the stone skip over the water.

RISING HAT

Wearing either a hat with a brim or a baseball cap backward, stand with your back to a wall. The brim of your hat must be perpendicular to the wall while touching it as well.

Place your thumb in your mouth and blow vigorously while you lean back against the wall with the brim of your hat touching the wall. This will exert pressure, which will raise your hat up off your head.

Although the blowing motion is just pretense, it will appear as if you have magically blown your hat off your head. Good timing is a necessity, so practice.

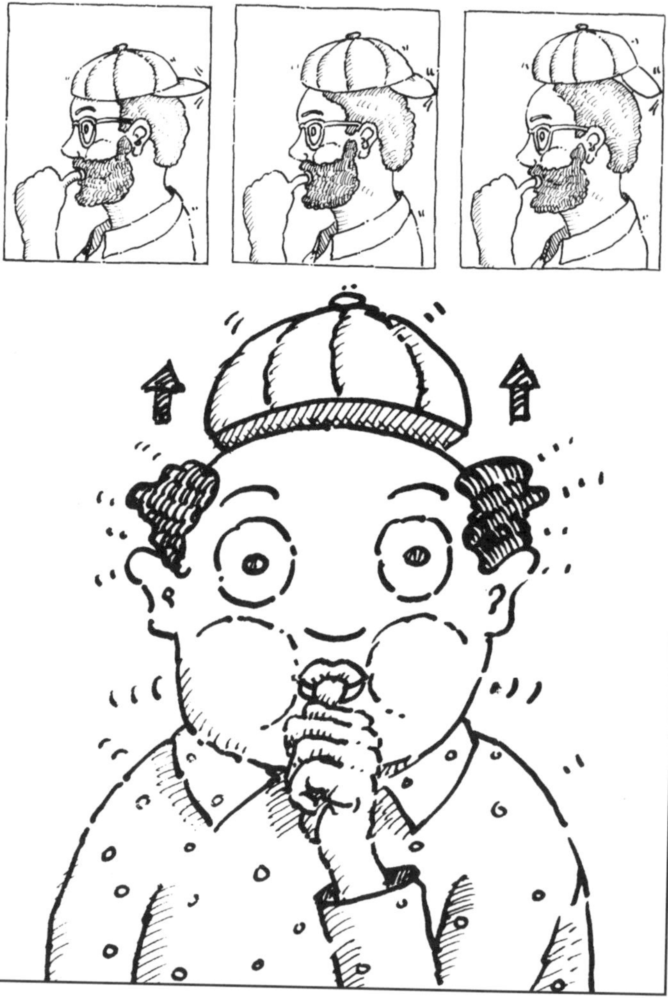

FUNNY
ARMS

Creating "funny" arms requires the participation of two people.

One person must stand or sit facing the audience with his arms held loosely behind his back.

The second person must stand or sit directly behind the first person and put his arms through the armpits of the first person. If possible, the second person should not be seen.

Upon first impression it will appear as though the arms that are seen belong to the person in front.

CLOUD
PICTURES

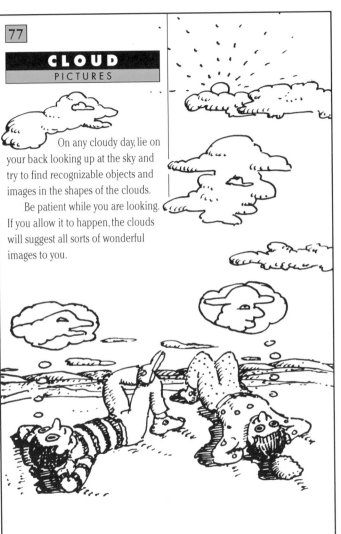

On any cloudy day, lie on your back looking up at the sky and try to find recognizable objects and images in the shapes of the clouds.

Be patient while you are looking. If you allow it to happen, the clouds will suggest all sorts of wonderful images to you.

BAG CATCHING TRICK

Hold a brown paper bag open by its top edge using only one hand with your index and middle fingers inside the bag and your thumb on the outside of the bag, facing your body.

With your free hand pretend to toss something up into the air, and using the bag, pretend to catch it by snapping your fingers through the bag which makes the appropriate sound, as if something fell into the bag.

You may facilitate this illusion by moving the bag around in the air in anticipation of where the tossed object will fall, while following the imaginary object with your eyes.

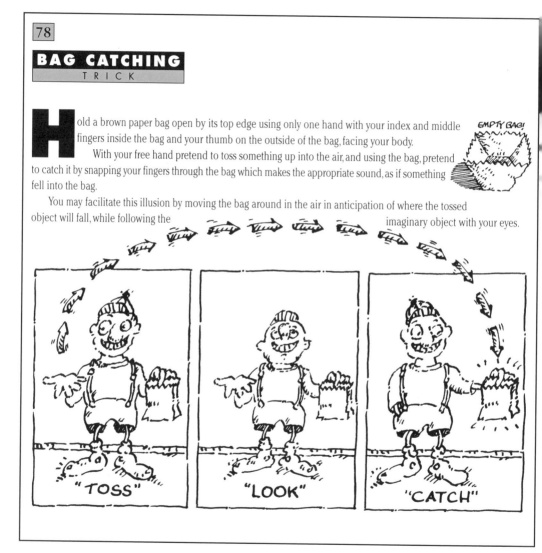

SALT SHAKER BALANCING

Using an old-fashioned salt shaker that is either six- or eight-sided, begin by spilling a small amount of salt on the table top.

Then slowly tilt the salt shaker to an approximate sixty-degree angle. Trying to get the salt shaker to stay in this position requires steady hands and patience. You must use both hands and gently move the salt shaker back and forth between your hands to try to find the correct angle for balancing. By slowly maneuvering the salt shaker around in the salted area, or spinning it slightly you are trying to find its center of gravity, which is the key to balancing a salt shaker.

When you have finally accomplished this feat, use a drinking straw to blow away the remaining salt carefully. Remember, it takes only a single grain of salt to accomplish this miracle.

80

BICYCLE
NOISEMAKER

All you need is a clothespin, a playing card or a baseball card, and a bicycle.

Attach the playing card onto the frame of your bicycle with the clothespin so that as you pedal the sound of the card hitting the spokes of your bicycle wheel will sound like a motor.

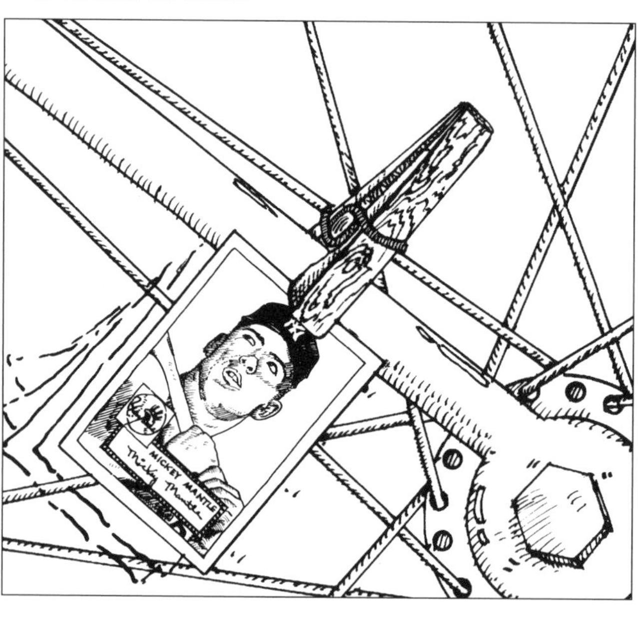

81

PAPER
AIRPLANE

Begin by folding a rectangular piece of paper in half, creating a fold line. Open the paper.

Then fold two of the corners into the center fold line, forming a point at one end.

Next fold each of the pointed ends in half toward the center fold line and turn the paper over and fold it in half.

Fold the wide end in half on each side, lifting both wide ends at a ninety-degree angle to the center fold.

Using your thumb and index finger hold the airplane beneath its wings near the center. It is now ready for takeoff. Toss it gently.

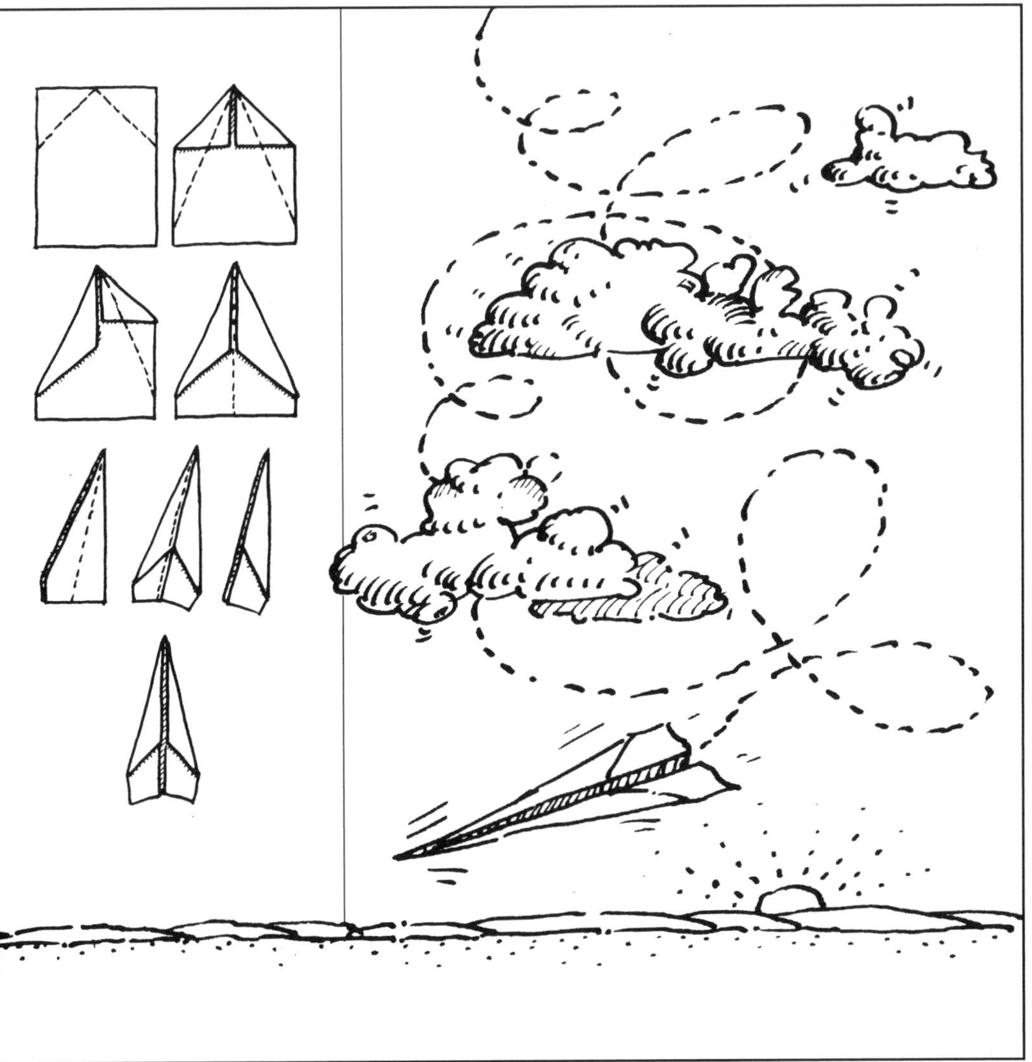

STRAW POPPING

"Straw popping" requires two people. One person must hold a plastic drinking straw comfortably at either end, then begin to wind the straw using both hands, until it knots. Continue winding until there is only an inch of smooth straw left in the center.

When the straw can't be wound any further, the person not holding the straw gets to pop it by forcefully flicking their finger at its center.

This will produce a loud and startling popping noise.

83

BENT FINGER
IN NOSE

Hold your hand with your index finger folded in, and all your other fingers standing straight up.

Your bent finger should face in toward your body and not be seen by the prospective audience. Line up your bent finger with the bottom of your nose and push the knuckle against the nostril. This must be done in front of a mirror to practice perfect form.

To the viewer it will appear as if your index finger is stuck in your nose.

84

CATCHING
QUARTERS

Bend one arm with your hand over your shoulder, palm facing up and your forearm perpendicular to your body.

Begin by using one quarter, which you will place on your forearm, approximately two inches from your elbow.

After you have balanced a quarter you must straighten your arm with a quick forward motion and as the quarter falls catch it with the same hand.

When you have perfected the movement of balancing and then catching one quarter, you can advance to using two, then three, then four, and so on.

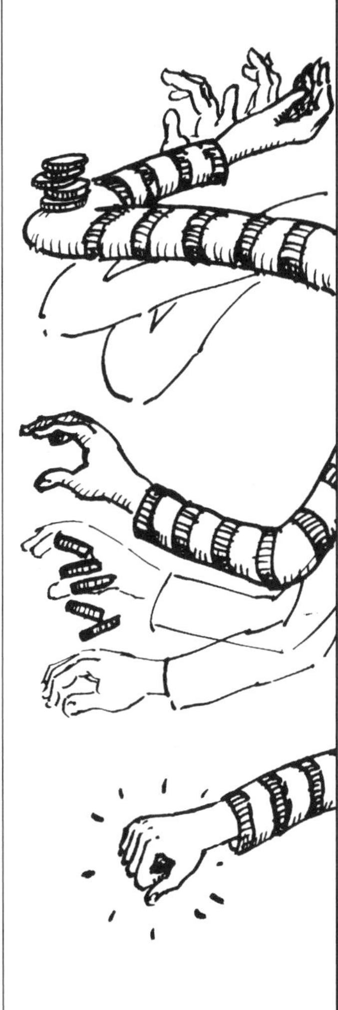

85

LAND O' LAKES™
FOLDED BOX

Using the box from a Land O'Lakes™ package, remove the side panels so the package can lie flat. Score the package as indicated on the diagram by scoring the top fold on the reverse side and the lower fold on the front side.

Now fold the box where you have scored it and you will be surprised by the change in the woman's anatomy.

86

MATCH
BOY

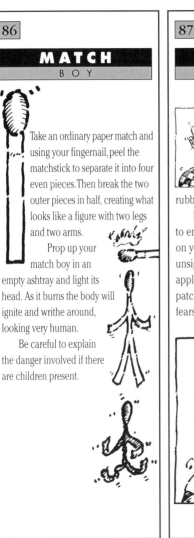

Take an ordinary paper match and using your fingernail, peel the matchstick to separate it into four even pieces. Then break the two outer pieces in half, creating what looks like a figure with two legs and two arms.

Prop up your match boy in an empty ashtray and light its head. As it burns the body will ignite and writhe around, looking very human.

Be careful to explain the danger involved if there are children present.

87

MONSTER
FACE

A monster face can be created by using either Scotch™ tape or rubber bands.

Large rubber bands may be used to encircle the head causing the skin on your face to bunch up in a most unsightly way. Scotch™ tape may be applied to the face creating a patchwork of skin that has a rather fearsome monster look to it.

88

RUBBER GLOVE
BALLOON

A rubber glove balloon can be created by blowing up a thin, unlined or surgical rubber glove and then tying the open end in a knot. If necessary use a string or a rubber band.

These balloons have a cartoon appearance similar to cow udders to them and make unusual party decorations.

89

ROCK PAPER SCISSORS

Rock Paper Scissors is a way of choosing who goes first, or who wins and loses, or who is "It."

It works this way: Rock is represented by your fist. Paper is when your hand is held open and your fingers are together. Scissors is represented by extending your index and middle fingers which are held open while your thumb holds your ring finger and pinkie tucked into your palm.

Each hand position is able to win over one other hand position as well as lose to one other hand position as follows: Rock crushes Scissors, but can be engulfed by Paper. Scissors cuts Paper, but can be crushed by Rock. Paper engulfs Rock, but can be cut by Scissors. That's what makes this perfectly fair.

When choosing, count aloud, one, two, three, shoot. On shoot, extend your hand and alternate between being Rock, Paper, and Scissors.

Choosing can be done between two or three people at a time. Two of the same equals a draw.

The positions are easy to assume and are visually memorable.

FINGER SEPARATION

This is a difficult posture to master. It will take patience and practice.

To begin, place your hand on a flat surface and separate your fingers between the middle finger and the ring finger, forming a **V** with your fingers.

Do this with both hands. When you have practiced and find you can accomplish this, then try it while your hands are raised in the air. Fingers must open to the **V** position in a single movement. Opening and closing your other fingers hurts the effect.

When you have perfected this, the advanced stage is to place your hands together with your palms facing and touching. Then try to separate your fingers in the same way.

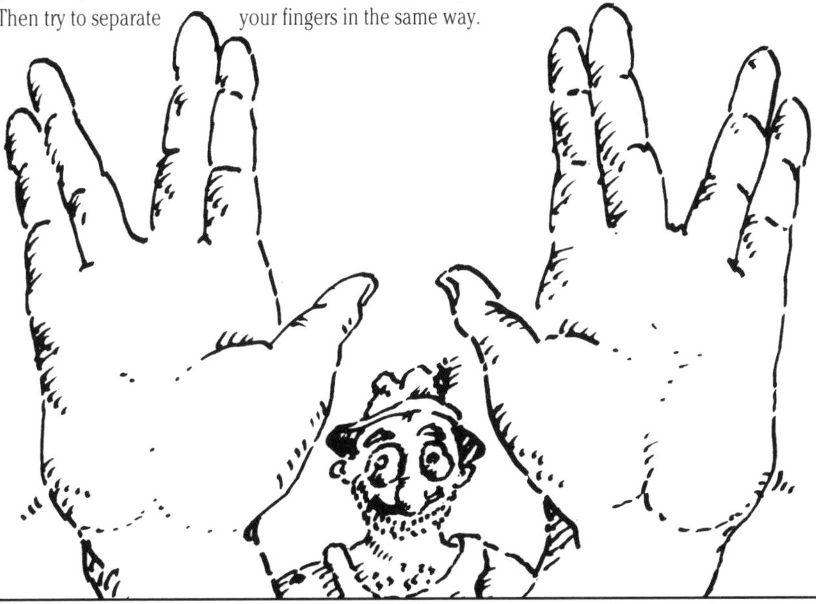

91

GUM WRAPPER
ROPE

To create a gum wrapper rope you need the paper wrappers from chewing gum packages. Begin by carefully opening the paper wrapper which comes folded in thirds and is sometimes lightly glued.

Fold the wrapper in half the long way, creating a long narrow rectangle. Press your fingernail along the fold to create a very flat, smooth crease.

Next refold the wrapper by turning it inside out and again pressing your fingernail along the edge, which re-creates a sharp fold line. Repeat this process at least two more times. Then tear apart the wrapper along the crease you have created. Tearing can be facilitated by holding one side of the fold down while pulling away the other side. This will produce two long rectangles of equal lengths and widths. These will each get folded in half lengthwise, twice—creating two very long and narrow rectangles.

Fold each thin rectangle in half, creating a **V**-shape. Then fold the lengths in half to the center of the **V**-shape. This creates a smaller, thicker **V**-shape.

Finally insert one **V**-shape through another with the open side facing up. This forms a thicker, entwined **V**-shape which can be added to again and again.

Remember always to keep the open end up otherwise the wrappers get stuck when you are trying to insert one through another.

This can be done with any rectangular pieces of paper of the same size, but using gum wrappers creates a most interesting design because of the placement of the words and colors which form new designs in the folding process.

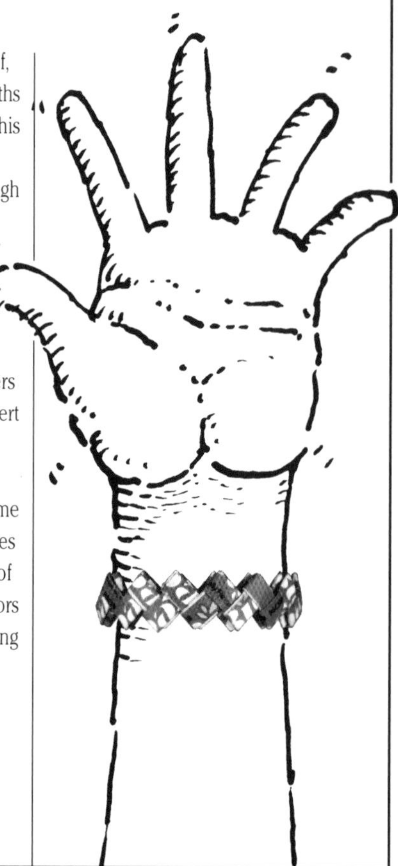

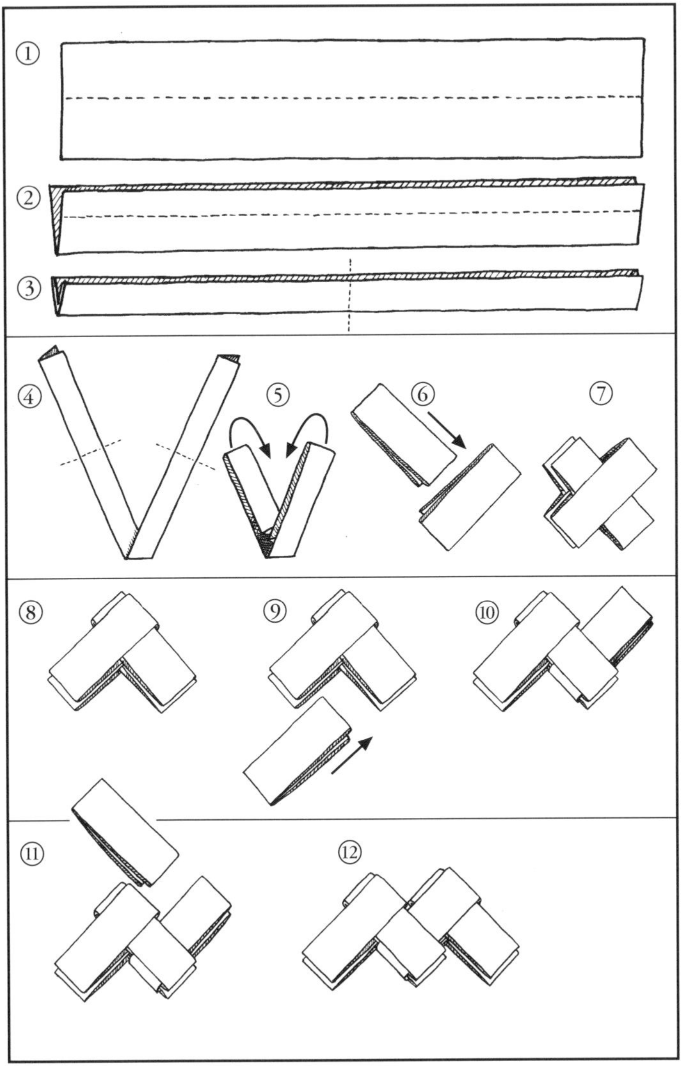

92

CHEEK NOISES

Puff out either one or both of your cheeks by trying to breathe out through your mouth while keeping your lips tightly closed.

Then using your hand or hands, gently pat your cheek or cheeks, which will produce some interesting and rude noises as the air is forced from your mouth.

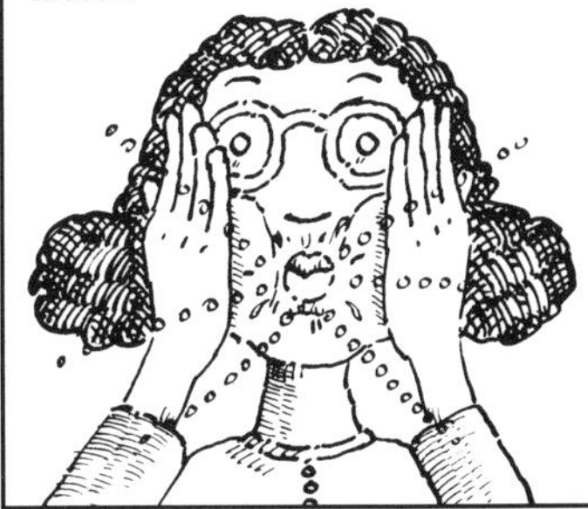

93

TALKING HAND

Make a fist with your thumb tucked into it, while keeping your fingers relaxed.

Next practice lowering and raising your thumb while it is in this horizontal tucked position.

You will see a resemblance to a mouth, with the thumb representing the lower lip.

To enhance the impression, draw a nose and eyes above the mouth, using skin paint, eye make-up, or lipstick. Then use your ventriloquist abilities to create words for your hand to speak.

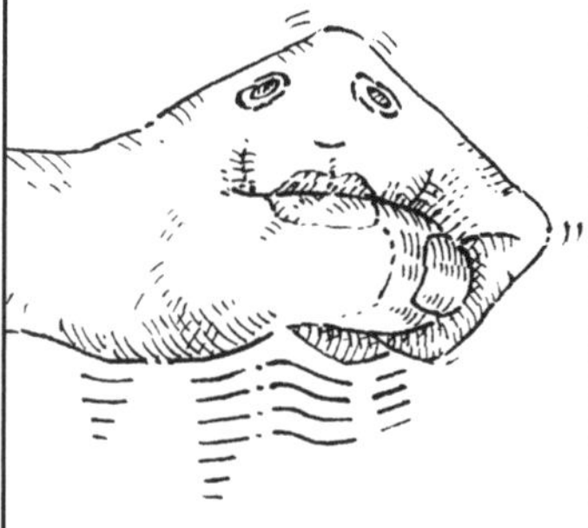

94

SNOWFLAKE CATCHING

Snowflake catching must be done with your tongue and can only be accomplished by standing outside during a snowfall with your head tilted back, while sticking your tongue out as far as you can.

One may either stand perfectly still, or rock back and forth, or bob and weave, or run in circles all with your tongue sticking out waiting for a snowflake to land.

This is not easy, and there are many techniques. But basically, one must be lucky.

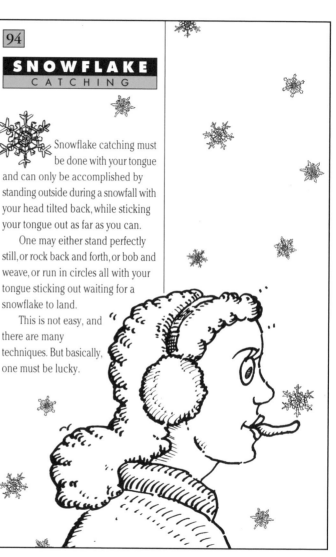

95

EMBARRASSING NOISEMAKER

Using a wire handle with cardboard tubing, normally used by department stores to facilitate the carrying of large packages, thread a rubber band across the metal bottom of the handle so that it is taut. If there is any slack, double the rubber band.

Next insert a small piece of cardboard,* approximately 1 - by -1¼ - inches, in the center of the rubber band and wind it by spinning it, making it as tight as possible.

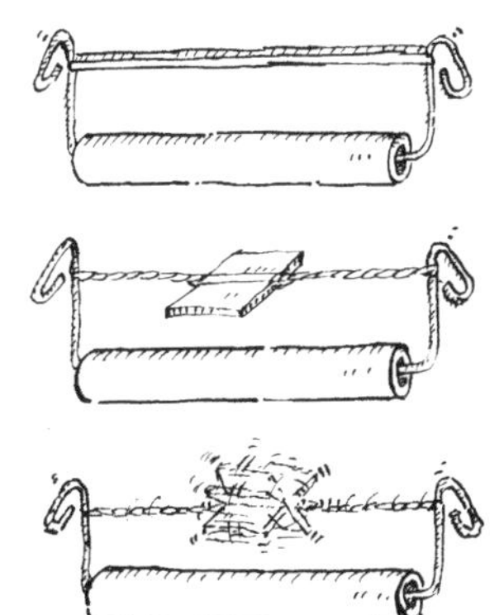

Then place the tightly wound apparatus beneath a seat cushion toward the front. Experiment with different cushions to find the one that works best.

Once your victim is seated, be patient. The embarrassing noisemaker is being compressed and will not do its job until the victim rises. Upon standing, the cushion will move upwards, releasing the noisemaker and a burst of sound will ensue.

*A button with large holes can be substituted for the piece of cardboard by threading it through the rubber band.

NEWSPAPER
HAT

A two-page spread from any newspaper is needed.

First fold the paper in half as it normally appears on the newsstand.

Then holding it horizontally, fold down first one corner to the center of the page, forming a large triangle, and then the other corner.

The bottom of one page of the newspaper that is not part of the triangle must be folded in half up to the bottom of the triangle's base and again so that it overlaps the bottom of the triangle, as if you are making a cuff. Then, do the same to the other half of the page.

The results will look like a pyramid with a brim which may be worn either sideways or facing front depending on one's sense of style.

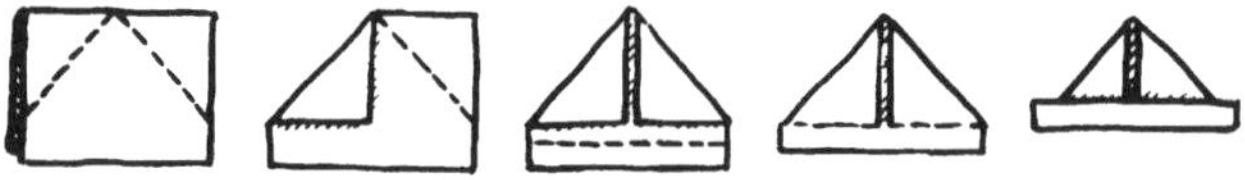

97

PAPER TUBE
LOUDSPEAKER

Take the cardboard tube from an empty roll of toilet paper or the cardboard tube from an empty paper towel roll. Place one of the open ends against your mouth and either speak, quack, hum, or make whatever sounds you wish into it.

The sound of your voice will be intensified as it exits from the other end of the tube.

98

HAND
FLUTE

Cup each hand and clap them together, keeping your fingers rounded. Line up your thumbs next to one another and blow into the thumbs, with your bottom lip beneath your knuckle and your top lip beneath your fingernails. Leave a small space beneath the knuckle for air to escape.

To accomplish this feat requires patience and practice. If done correctly, you will hear a whistling sound which you can vary by raising and lowering the fingers on your outside hand. Doing this will change the notes and simulate the sound of a flute.

99

LOVES ME
LOVES ME NOT

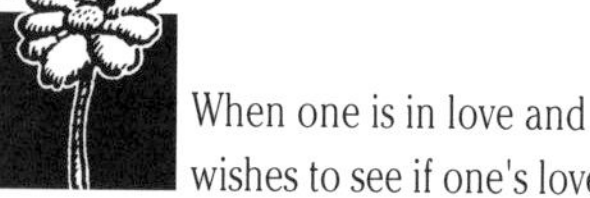

When one is in love and wishes to see if one's love is reciprocated, the following ritual is often enacted.

The daisy is a common flower with petals which are usually either yellow or white.

Pick a daisy and, holding it by its stem, remove the petals one at a time while saying, "She/he loves me," accompanied by removing another petal then saying, "she/he loves me not," followed by removing another petal and so on, until the daisy has one petal left. The last petal indicates whether you are loved or not.

100

HAND
SHADOWS

Hand shadows are best created in any darkened room where there is a single light source that you can shine on a wall while placing your hands directly in the path of the light. The shadow is caused by your hands interrupting the beam of light.

There are innumerable shadows to be made but one of the most popular resembles a bird. Keep your hands open with your palms facing your body, cross your arms at your wrists and overlap your thumbs. Flutter your hands and the bird will be flapping its wings. You can also make appropriate sound effects.

101

CAT'S
CRADLE

Cat's cradle is probably one of the oldest activities that has been handed down from generation to generation.

It is done with a piece of string or yarn that is knotted, forming a continuous loop approximately forty inches long.

One begins by looping the string around each of one's hands just beneath the fingers.

Then insert the opposite hand's middle finger under the string which is crossing the palm, pull it back toward the opposite palm. This forms the letter **X** on both sides of the string.

A second person is required to remove this cradle of string, transferring it to his hands.

The cradle is passed back and forth creating different configurations and using different finger positions until someone tires.

In keeping with tradition, the magic of cat's cradle must be passed down by an initiate.